Ready to Share One Bread

Ready to Share
One Bread
Preparing children for Holy Communion

Nick Harding and Sandra Millar

First published in Great Britain in 2015

Society for Promoting Christian Knowledge
36 Causton Street
London SW1P 4ST
www.spckpublishing.co.uk

British Library Cataloguing-in-Publication Data
A catalogue record for this book is available from the British Library

ISBN 978–0–281–07053–4
eBook ISBN 978–0–281–07054–1

Typeset by Graphicraft Limited, Hong Kong
First printed in Great Britain by Ashford Colour Press
Subsequently digitally printed in Great Britain

eBook by Graphicraft Limited, Hong Kong

Produced on paper from sustainable forests

Contents

Part 1
The story so far

Part 2
Preparing the ground

Part 3
Preparing the people

Part 4
Joining in

Part 5
Carrying on

Contributors

Nick Harding is Children's Ministry Adviser for the Diocese of Southwell and Nottingham, where he has advised many parishes on admitting children to Holy Communion, among other issues. He is a member of the Church of England's General Synod and is a well-known conference speaker and trainer.

The Revd Dr Sandra Millar is Head of Projects and Development for the Church of England, where she oversees projects on the Church's engagement with those coming for weddings, baptisms and funerals. She was previously Adviser for Work with Children and Families in the Diocese of Gloucester, where she supported parishes in their work with children, including advising on admission to Holy Communion and school Eucharists. Prior to that she was a vicar in the Dorchester-on-Thames team ministry and a curate in Barnet: she has also worked in marketing.

The Revd Dr Steve Dixon is Children's Work Officer for the Diocese of Manchester. He holds a professional doctorate in children's ministry, for which he researched the effects experienced by Christian adults when nurturing children.

The Rt Revd Michael Perham has recently retired as Bishop of Gloucester. He is the author of several books for SPCK, including *Jesus and Peter*, *To Tell Afresh*, *Glory in our Midst* and, with Paula Gooder, *Echoing the Word: The Bible in the Eucharist*.

Foreword

The four-year-old had a determined look on his face: 'Does Jesus love me?' he asked.

'Yes, you know he does,' replied the smiling vicar. The four-year-old took hold of a piece of the bread the vicar held in her hand and said, 'Well, this Jesus doesn't, as I'm not allowed to share him.' It hurt the vicar deeply and, soon after, she shared the story with me.

All 25 of us were squeezed around the extended table; in front of us was a table heaving with everything you could hope for in a traditional Christmas dinner. The youngest was just a few months old; the eldest in her early eighties. Almost every decade in between was represented. It was a glorious celebration. There was a wholeness about it because of the presence of every family member. Memories were shared of previous celebrations when others no longer alive were present. The story rolled on; remembrance, continuity, newness and hope for the future were all expressed around the common table. Yes, it was unique to have everyone there at the same time, but it was a family at one.

Holy Communion is all about celebrating, remembering and being God's family together. Its focus is on the Lord who instituted it; it is his gift to us. He commanded us to do it in remembrance of him. He told us it was to remain until the great banquet yet to come. He set it in the context of a meal eaten together. It is the Lord's Supper.

I have been convinced for a long time that children should be taking a full part in this central celebration of our worship and discipleship. They are full-blown members of the Church through baptism. They have gifts given by God for the building up of the whole Church. They have spiritual insights that we all need to heed. Yes, they have much to learn and understand, but so do people of all ages. They do not grasp all that is going on, but neither do adults.

So material that helps everyone to understand Holy Communion is always welcome. The great gift that Sandra and Nick bring is their breadth of experience and knowledge. They both have much first-hand experience of working with children, leading worship for all God's people, and helping adults work better with children. They have also seen lots of other people in action, across all traditions and styles within the Church, and drawn from that experience. They are enormously well placed to help. In this book, they have taken that wealth and offered a table full of goodies that we can all enjoy.

One of the delights of the book is that you can read it from beginning to end or you can dip into it at different times. It is intensely practical, covering every aspect of questions that arise regarding children and communion. It is a privilege to be able to commend it.

May our family celebrations of the Eucharist be truly thanksgiving meals where those of all ages are welcome, and, in them, may we all know that we are deeply loved by God, for Jesus has welcomed us to his table.

The Rt Revd Paul Butler,
Bishop of Durham

Acknowledgements

I would like to thank all the churches in the Diocese of Southwell and Nottingham, and people at training events across England, who have shared their experiences with me and have helped me to develop my thinking.

Nick Harding

With thanks to all those churches and church leaders who shared their thoughts, ideas and experiences, and were willing to try new things.

Sandra Millar

Introduction

Sandra Millar

The first time I worked with a parish to explore and admit children to communion before confirmation was in 2001. It was such a new idea for us that we took a long time to think, to pray and to discuss, supported by the Diocesan Children's Officer (which is always a good place to look for advice and help). The issue was being discussed widely at the time, but for us it acquired a new urgency when a family returning to England from the USA joined us. In the Episcopal Church of the USA, children receive communion at an early age – so the children in the family began to take communion with us. That started the questions and the concerns.

Over a few months we had open meetings, preached sermons, wrote articles in the parish magazines and had an amazing day for adults and children together to explore the meaning of Holy Communion. That day involved group discussions in age groups, activities that helped all of us think about what communion meant to us, and ended with an opportunity to share reflections. I can still remember the feelings of surprise in the room as we heard children from seven and upwards sharing deep insights into their faith.

Eventually the PCCs made a decision, took a vote, obtained the necessary permission from the bishop and we moved to the next stage. We invited the group, aged between seven and twelve years old, to a series of six sessions on Sunday afternoons. Then, on an ordinary Sunday morning, that group were admitted to communion. I remember praying for them and giving each of them a special book, and then remember how it very quickly became ordinary within the life of the church for children to receive communion with us. We worked with small groups of children about twice a year, and also prepared some of the older ones for confirmation a couple of years later.

That confirmation group, made up of youngsters aged 11–15, some of whom had been admitted to communion earlier and some of whom were following a more traditional route through confirmation, was very interesting. As they sat around on the floor discussing what it meant to live as Christians, what it meant to be part of a church, I was struck by the maturity of those who had been receiving communion for the past year or more. It really seemed that they had a clear sense of belonging to a faith community and a clear sense of being Christian. Of course, I may be looking back with rose-tinted spectacles, but I was recently greatly encouraged when I had one of those unexpected random encounters with someone, and heard that one of that first group of children is now a church musician and worship leader.

Since then I have had the opportunity to work with many different parishes who embark on this process – and the questions and concerns remain remarkably similar. Congregations are often puzzled when a vicar raises the question, often when there is a new incumbent, or a new family, who is bringing experience from a different context. Almost inevitably there is a resistance to change, a sense that this is something out of the ordinary. But some things have changed over the years: there is a greater confidence about approaching the issue, and often a real desire to reach out to children in church and community.

And that is a really good place to start. It's tempting to begin with the process and the practicalities, but taking time to think about children's experience of church and to reflect on what is currently happening in church with, for and around them is always worthwhile. It's a good idea to articulate a desire to see children grow in faith as disciples of Jesus, whatever the outcome of discussions about communion. Time spent thinking about children and church, exploring some of the more recent thinking about children's spirituality, can provide a really good basis for more formal discussion (for example, Rebecca Nye's book, *Children's Spirituality*,[1] would make a good book for a small group to study).

At some point there is a need to go further – to think about the Church of England's processes and to discover some of the history and theology around the question. Some parishes move quickly through this, perhaps with an article or a sermon, or a discussion at the PCC. But others take more time to explore the issues – once I was invited to take part in an open debate, with speakers both for and against the question! Different people are interested in different aspects around the issue – some want to know all about the practicalities, others find the history really helpful while yet others will want to look at biblical and theological issues. The key is to make sure everyone has an opportunity to find out what is going on and to ask questions – even if they don't take that opportunity. Don't forget to check out the process in your own diocese – there does need to be a formal vote at a PCC and permission granted from the bishop before any change in practice happens.

Once all the discussion has taken place and the parish is moving ahead, those who work alongside children and families need to think about how to help them get ready. Not every child in the church may want to take communion, and not all parents will be sure about what it involves – even after all the good communication and information. There may be more complex family situations that require careful pastoral care even before any programme begins. If there are children who have not yet been baptized (and it might be that this has never come up previously), then different conversations need to happen, helping those children and families decide if that is right for them.

Choosing the right programme can be difficult – there are several available and it's important to think about the resources that you have available and the time that families can commit as you decide how to approach this. Families have increasingly demanding lives – children have classes and clubs to go to in the week and after-school friends may live at a distance. At the weekend, families often have to catch up with different generations in different places as well as with all the chores and tasks of family life, to say nothing of catching up with each

other – or even catching their breath! Asking for a regular commitment for six or more weeks can be quite challenging, depending on your context and community, although it can be a great opportunity to build a real sense of belonging. The courses that are available may need adapting to reflect the theology and practice in your church, so time is needed for the leaders to think it through, to plan and to pray. The course in this book is short and designed for the whole family to do together, which is a different approach, and can fit in well with contemporary family life.

Once the children have thought through communion, there will come a day when they receive bread and wine for the first time. This is not the end of the process – it is just the beginning of a lifetime of discovering all that it means to share one bread, to be a follower of Jesus and be part of his people. This is a good time to review how children in church are involved with worship, and especially to think about how they are going to be part of a eucharistic community. It might also be an opportunity to help the whole congregation reflect on some of these questions, helping everyone to remember that the presence of Jesus in bread and wine is a gift and a mystery, however long we have been sharing. Again, this is something where there is a lot of help available – through diocesan advisers or through online resources and newsletters.

Recently the Church of England approved two additional Eucharistic Prayers for use when the majority of those present are children – *Common Worship: Additional Eucharistic Prayers*.[2] These prayers have a fresh language style and are very much written with the idea that children will be involved in helping to create the worship service where they are used, and will be joining in with the prayer itself. The prayers were born from a particular context – the context of a school Eucharist – and they work very well. Many church schools, independent, state, primary, secondary, have found that a regular whole school, year group or class service of Holy Communion is a key marker in their calendar. On the few occasions I have been present at a school Eucharist it has always been inspiring and moving, with lots of participation, lots of seriousness and a real sense of community.

It's from all of these experiences that this book has slowly taken shape.

This is a book with a heart – at its heart is a desire to see the whole church family sharing, learning and worshipping together. It's that desire that has taken all of the authors and contributors on a journey. For some of us it's been a theological journey, whereas for others it's been a immensely practical. Wherever you and your church family are on the journey of exploring children taking communion before confirmation, there will be something for you in this book

How to use this book

For most books the starting point is really obvious – you start at the beginning and work through to the end. But *Ready to Share One Bread* doesn't have to be used that way. You can jump straight to Chapter 6 and look at a course for preparing children, or you can start at the end if you want to go further, and begin exploring the Eucharist as part of school life. It is a complete resource, designed to help you think about the decision, prepare the whole church, worship together and then go on with your faith journey as a community.

The book is arranged in five parts, which are discussed sequentially below, under 'What's in this book?'. But depending on how you like to learn and explore, you might prefer to follow different routes into the book.

- If you want to get to the practical resources, you will need to look at:
  - Chapter 4 – how to explore children and communion with your parish;
  - Chapter 6 – a two-part course for helping children and families prepare to receive communion;
  - Chapter 8 – an outline service for admitting children to communion;
  - Chapter 9 – more resources and ideas;
  - Chapter 12 – ideas and resources for continuing the journey of discipleship.
- If you want to read how things work out in practice then you will need:
  - Chapter 3 – how one parish went through the process;
  - Chapter 5 – how parishes tried out the all-age approach to preparing children;
  - Chapter 11 – taking the Eucharist beyond Sunday.
- If you want to explore the background and go further then you will need:
  - Chapters 1 and 2 – the history and current practice of the Church of England;
  - Chapter 7 – what it means for eucharistic worship to include everyone;
  - Chapter 10 – what difference it makes for children in their journey.

What's in this book?

As mentioned above, the book is arranged in five parts, and taken together it offers all the material a parish needs.

Part 1: The story so far looks at the current situation in the Church of England regarding the admission of children to communion before confirmation. It's an opportunity to look at the history and to discover how this 'new' approach is connected to the Church through history and culture. Chapter 1, by Bishop Michael Perham, offers a brief theology of children and the Eucharist, highlighting different theological reflections, looking at Scripture, and the journey that the Church of England has taken in recent years. In Chapter 2 Nick Harding goes further into the past, looking at past practice and thinking before bringing it up to the present day. For many church leaders and congregations, discovering the connections across time and place is a key to beginning the discussions.

Thinking about children and communion is not just an intellectual issue. When people begin to discuss the idea there is often a lot of emotional response. Opinions are expressed and questions are asked as adults and children alike try to think around something they may never have considered before. **Part 2: Preparing the ground** is the practical starting point for churches beginning to explore the questions. In Chapter 3 Nick Harding presents the story of a church as it considers the admission of children to communion. There are different opinions and there are different ideas – just as there will be in most churches. The chapter describes how one church used the processes to help everyone share their views and then arrive at a decision.

In Chapter 4 Nick offers material for exploring the issue with the whole congregation, with discussion questions, material for Bible study and practical ideas for reflection. There are a range of different approaches and clear guidelines as to how to use them, so that a parish congregation has an opportunity to think deeply. Whatever decision is made, everyone will have explored the Eucharist in new ways.

In **Part 3: Preparing the people** you will find new material to help children prepare to receive communion before confirmation. Since the admission of children to communion before confirmation was first explored there have been many schemes and programmes, and different things work for different churches. This course is short – it only takes place over two sessions, and it tries to avoid an overly 'educational' approach, offering lots of activities and interaction. It is also designed for adults and children to do together, whether at home or with the church family. Chapter 5 describes how people felt when they used this material, their hesitations and their discoveries.

Chapter 6 is the course itself, with everything you need to run the two sessions.

Once the children have spent some time thinking about communion, there comes a time when they will take communion for the first time and then be part of regular eucharistic worship. **Part 4: Joining in** has lots of principles and practical ideas about making worship accessible to all ages, particularly thinking about children and the Eucharist. There are ideas for helping everyone take part in the liturgy, creative ways to approach prayer and a whole raft of practical ways children can help.

Chapter 7 explores the principles and Chapter 8 includes a complete liturgy to use on any Sunday when children are to be admitted to communion, complete with a talk as well as ideas for readings and prayers. There are lots of additional ideas in Chapter 9, which can be used at special services or on Sundays throughout the year.

Being admitted to communion is not the end of the process – it is simply a stage on the journey of faith and discipleship which is life-long. **Part 5: Carrying on** goes beyond the discussions and the practicalities, and beyond Sunday worship, to start exploring the difference it makes to be part of a eucharistic community. In Chapter 10 Steve Dixon draws on his research to explore the way taking communion affects and changes children. Finally, in Chapter 11 Nick Harding returns to some real stories about the impact the admission of children to communion makes on the wider church community.

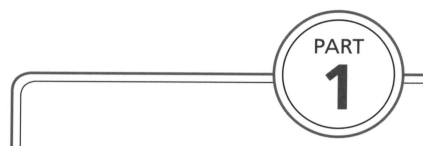

PART

1

The story so far

Why it matters

A brief theology of children and the Eucharist

Michael Perham

'Why can't I have some?'

It is the question that clergy have heard over and over again at the altar rail. Fortunately for them, the question is more often posed to mum or dad rather than the priest. I'm always grateful for that, for I know no satisfactory answer to the question. If it would not cause pastoral confusion I would reply, 'There is no reason why you can't. Put out your hand. Jesus wants to feed you.' If I'm honest, that's what I most want to say to the adults who come to the altar, having been well instructed that, because they are not confirmed, they cannot be communicants and so bow their heads for a blessing. 'Put out your hand. Jesus wants to feed you' is something I would like to say almost every time I preside at the Eucharist. The fundamental issue is not so much about children as about all those whom we exclude from the Lord's table.

But, of course, it is not as simple as that. I'm not sure the theology itself is very much more complicated. Jesus wanting to feed us is very fundamental. But certainly church practice has made it a good deal more complicated and we need to explore some of that if we are to find a more adequate answer to the question.

For the Church of England the move towards admitting children to Holy Communion really goes back to what is usually called 'The Ely Report'. Properly titled *Christian Initiation: Birth and Growth in the Christian Society*,[1] it was produced by a commission chaired by Ted Roberts, then the Bishop of Ely, and published in 1971, more than 40 years ago. It was a seminal work and still shapes Church of England understanding of the relationship between baptism, confirmation and first communion. Not everything that it claims is accepted by every

Anglican, or even every Anglican liturgist, but it has shaped both the creation of liturgical rites and ongoing pastoral practice for nearly two generations. At heart it teaches that baptism is complete initiation into the Christian community. There is nothing more that has to be done before a person is fully a member of the Church. The Ely Report summarizes its understanding of baptism in this way:

> Baptism is the effectual sign of the union of the Church and thereby of the individual with Christ... This baptismal union with Christ is continually renewed and sustained by Holy Communion to which Baptism itself looks forward and for which it is the only sacramental prerequisite.

It goes on to recommend that 'the Church should make explicit its recognition of baptism as the full and complete rite of Christian initiation'.

This leads the report to be clear that confirmation is not essentially part of Christian initiation. Instead it sees it as a pastoral rite and a declaration of mature Christian discipleship.

> Confirmation has often been regarded in the past as in some cases the completion of Christian initiation. We believe that Confirmation signifies far more than an isolated rite important though that is; it is also a focal point in an on-going ministry of training. We propose that this vital element of training should now receive the widest possible recognition, and thus *restore to Confirmation its true function of fostering the spiritual growth of the individual Christian*. This on-going ministry should include admission to Communion where the circumstances warrant this at an earlier age than is normally considered normal.

The report thus makes admission to communion something separate from confirmation, or at least not necessarily attached to it. It goes on to set out some principles relating to admission to communion.

We believe that it should be permissible to admit baptised Christians to Communion after preparation without using Confirmation as some kind of a preliminary spiritual or educational qualification. As the right of Confirmation ceases to be no more than a conventional gateway to Communion, so its significance will be enhanced, as it becomes an act of personal commitment and commissioning at an age when such an act becomes truly meaningful.

Communion will now become a means of grace and strengthening for those involved in the Church's on-going ministry of training, rather than a goal to be attained at the conclusion of a course of instruction. *Every person, however, must be carefully prepared to receive the sacrament in accordance with his own capabilities.*

First Communion should be an occasion of the greatest importance. It should be administered whenever possible by the bishop, thus ensuring for each newly admitted communicant direct contact with him.

Concerning admission to Communion, we recommend that:

1   *It is permissible for the parish priest, at his discretion, to admit persons to Communion (if they so desire) who have been baptised with water in the name of the Trinity.*

2   *Adequate preparation for admission to Communion be provided and be such as to enable the candidates to participate in the Eucharist.*

3   *The first Communion be administered, wherever possible, by the bishop.*

It took from 1971 to 1997, 26 years, for policy to turn into practice, and even then the new practice was by way of exception, with communion following confirmation remaining the norm, as it still is today. In 1996 the House of Bishops produced Guidelines, the General Synod endorsed them and they were issued in a revised form in 1997. With little difference the Guidelines were turned into Regulations in 2006.

It is worth, at this point, pausing to explore the practice of the Orthodox and the Roman Catholic Churches, for they throw some light on Anglican understanding and practice. The Orthodox approach has a wonderful simplicity about it. Baptism includes anointing with the oil of chrism (which is regarded as the equivalent of the laying on of the bishop's hand in Anglican confirmation). Baptism is regarded as complete initiation. The newly baptized, however young, is immediately eligible for Holy Communion and may receive it from a spoon. Nothing further is needed as part of a process of becoming fully a member of the Church. An Orthodox child does not, therefore, receive preparation or training to be a communicant, nor does such a child remember their first communion, any more than they remember their first meal at home. They grow up simply as a member of a community that eats and drinks together.

The position in the Roman Catholic Church is not so simple. Children are admitted to communion before confirmation, but confirmation is still regarded as a sacramental stage in an initiation process. Confirmation, which may be by a priest, rather than by the bishop, involves anointing with the oil of chrism consecrated by the bishop. There is a recognition that baptism makes a person, of whatever age, a complete member of the Church, but the Catechism teaches that confirmation 'renders the bond with the Church more perfect'. There is no automatic granting of communicant status through baptism. Instead it comes, after preparation for first communion, usually at the age of seven or eight.

In many ways it seems that the Church of England, where it has admitted children to communion, has accepted the theology of the Orthodox Churches, but then adopted the practice of the Roman Catholic Church, with admission after preparation at the age of seven or eight as the norm.

It is now time to explore the 2006 Regulations. It is important to understand that first communion after confirmation remains the norm. Admission of children to communion is a permissible variant from the norm as expressed in the Book of Common Prayer and the canons, which enshrine the Church's doctrine. Nevertheless, under the Regulations, a baptized child may be admitted to communion provided that:

- the bishop directs that the practice may extend to his diocese;

- the parish priest has applied to the bishop for one or more of his or her parishes for the parish to admit children to communion;

- the Parochial Church Council of the parish has resolved to support the application;

- the bishop is satisfied that there is sufficient preparation and provision for future nurture in place in the parish and that the parish will encourage the child later to come to confirmation;

- that the parents of the child are content that the child shall be admitted;

- that the admission to communion is recorded in a register and the child given written evidence of admission.

The House of Bishops' Regulations do not specify at which age the child may be admitted, simply requiring the bishop to satisfy himself 'that the parish concerned has made adequate provision for preparation and continuing nurture in the Christian life'. This lack of guidance about age does, inevitably, lead to greater confusion in the Church. First there is the variety of practice whereby some children are admitted to communion before confirmation and some are not. But second there is the variety whereby, in one diocese, they may be admitted as young as aged three or four, while in another it might be seven or eight. To that must be added the further confusion that, in some dioceses, an admission to communion policy has not altered the willingness of the bishop to confirm a child aged as young as nine or ten, while in another, where the policy is in place, confirmation is always delayed until sixteen or over as a kind of adult commissioning. The present position is something of a mess.

In order to try to bring some order out of this pastoral and liturgical chaos, we need to go back to the New Testament and the early centuries. But first it may be useful to reflect on how many of the Ely

Report recommendations have been implemented and which have disappeared.

1   In general the understanding of baptism as complete initiation has been accepted.

2   While communion after confirmation remains the norm, baptism cannot be seen as consistently the 'only sacramental prerequisite' for communicant status.

3   The permissibility of admitting baptized Christians to communion after preparation without confirmation has been established, but not as the norm.

4   Liturgical presidency by the bishop of admission to communion has been firmly resisted (not least lest it become confused with confirmation), but the bishop's involvement has been retained because the policy must have his approval and application to adopt it must be made to him.

5   There has been no great change in popular perception of confirmation. Its significance as an act of personal commitment and commissioning has not received fresh emphasis.

6   The Ely Report speaks consistently of admitting 'baptized Christians'. Current regulations on admission to communion are restricted to baptized children, not adults.

So it is clear both that the 1971 Ely Report remains the foundation of much Church of England thinking, but that its intentions have not yet been fully realized. More significantly, the Church has still not made up its mind to detach admission to communion from confirmation, let alone to attach it firmly to baptism without any further requirements.

Both the Ely Report and the Bishops' Regulations make much of 'preparation'. They assume that reception of communion is not simply a matter of sharing naturally in the Church's eucharistic meal, but requires preparation. The Ely Report calls it 'training'. It is this that has led bishops to set the minimum age limit at something between the ages of four and eight. A child capable of learning at school is also capable of learning about eucharistic participation. But there is, of course, a question about whether sharing the Lord's Supper is something that requires intellectual preparation. Clean hands and a pure heart might be sufficient.

Where might Scripture lead us? The teaching of Jesus does not resolve the matter for us. What it does do is to show that Jesus took children seriously and recognized that they are very much part of the kingdom of heaven.

In Mark 10.13–16 (which is reflected also in Matthew 19.13–15 and Luke 18.15–17), Jesus says:

> People were bringing little children to [Jesus] in order that he might touch them; and the disciples spoke sternly to them. But when Jesus saw this, he was indignant and said to them, 'Let the little children come to me; do not stop them; for it is to such as these that the kingdom of God belongs. Truly I tell you, whoever does not receive the kingdom of God as a little child will never enter it.' And he took them up in his arms, laid his hands on them, and blessed them.

'Let the children come to me,' says Jesus. It is not an explicit invitation to share in the Eucharist, though it is an affirmation of their place in the kingdom of God, and that kingdom is sometimes described as a place of feasting.

In the previous chapter Jesus has spoken about welcome. 'Whoever wants to be first must be last of all and servant of all,' he says.

> Then he took a little child and put it among them; and taking it in his arms, he said to them, 'Whoever welcomes one such child in my name welcomes me, and whoever welcomes me welcomes not me but the one who sent me.'
> (Mark 9.36–37)

Again the context is not a meal, but the plea is for the welcome of children. And a few verses later, he adds:

> If any of you put a stumbling-block before one of these little ones who believe in me, it would be better for you if a great millstone were hung around your neck and you were thrown into the sea.
> (Mark 9.42)

The message is reinforced; nothing and nobody must keep a child from Jesus. But it is Matthew, rather than Mark, who in his account of the feeding of the five thousand makes the only explicit reference to Jesus feeding children.

> All ate and were filled; and they took up what was left over of the broken pieces, twelve baskets full. And those who ate were about five thousand men, besides women and children.
> (Matthew 14.20–21)

He says the same about the feeding of the four thousand (Matthew 15.38). It is John, in his account of the feeding of the multitude, who introduces another element. Here it is a child who provides the wherewithal for the feast.

> One of his disciples, Andrew, Simon Peter's brother, said to him, 'There is a boy here who has five barley loaves and two fish.'
> (John 6.8–9)

It is inconceivable that, having brought the bread, the child would have been denied a share in it. But this is not the account of the Last Supper and, despite the fact that John sets the story within the chapter in which he explores the teaching about Jesus as the Bread of Life, people differ in the extent that they reckon this to have been a quasi-eucharistic occasion. Is Jesus doing something very different here from what he does in the upper room the night before his death?

For that occasion has a much more exclusive feel to it. In the upper room the evangelists are insistent that the meal was with 'the twelve'. No mention of other disciples, no mention of a woman, not even the mother of Jesus, and certainly no mention of a child. If we regard the Last Supper account as a controlling story in relation to the Eucharist, we have no explicit justification for the inclusion of children from within the Gospels. But nor do we have any explicit reason to exclude them. After all, if absence from the Last Supper meant exclusion from the Eucharist, it would also exclude all women and, according to some theology, all laity. The Last Supper does not settle the issue.

As for the rest of the New Testament, we have nothing that tells us who participated in the breaking of bread in the apostolic communities. We know that whole households were baptized together, among them the family of Cornelius the Centurion (Acts 10.48). It seems unlikely that any of those baptized would have been excluded from the meal in which they remembered Jesus. More problematic is what Paul writes in 1 Corinthians.

Having described the meal at which Jesus instituted the Eucharist (and it is the earliest account that we have), Paul writes:

> Whoever, therefore, eats the bread or drinks the cup of the Lord in an unworthy manner will be answerable for the body and blood of the Lord. Examine yourselves, and only then eat of the bread and drink of the cup. For all who eat and drink without discerning the body, eat and drink judgement against themselves.
>
> (1 Corinthians 11.27–29)

It is this passage, more than any other, that has led to an emphasis on preparation, training and teaching before people may receive Holy Communion. They must know what they are doing. They must, perhaps, understand. What exactly does 'discerning the body' or, in another text, 'discerning the Lord's body' mean? It could mean the communicant grasping that the bread is Christ's body and the wine is his blood. Or 'discerning the body' could mean understanding the nature of the Church and your own participation in it. If the former, it suggests a degree of understanding of the meaning of the Eucharist. And, indeed, an argument sometimes advanced against admitting children to communion is that they are too young to understand. I confess that this argument does not begin to convince me. The Eucharist is a wonderful mystery. The older that I get, the more that I participate in it, the more I value it, but I don't understand it more. I think I understand it less, but I am drawn more deeply into its mystery. I believe children can be drawn into it too whatever they do or do not understand.

As for the latter argument, children have a natural sense of belonging and of their own belonging, whether in the family that shares food at home or the larger family that shares food around the altar. I concede that Paul in 1 Corinthians, and Paul in 1 Corinthians alone, makes me hesitate and just

to begin to go with the discipline of admitting children to communion only at an age when they can discuss it. But in the end I am not convinced. Growing up having always shared the family meal, and not remembering the first time, seems as right for what we do in church as what we do at home.

Anglicans, Orthodox and Roman Catholics have always been clear that admission to communion should not precede baptism. This has not always been so in some of the evangelical churches and now it is being challenged in emerging churches and, to some extent, in Anglicanism. The challenge arises, not specifically in relation to children, but to anyone, adult or child, sharing in worship where there is an open table. That is a separate and different debate, but one that the Church has to have. But for the time being it is clear that the children we are speaking of welcoming to communion are those who have been baptized simply because it is their baptism that qualifies them, makes them members of the body.

The present very flexible and very confusing policy of the Church of England on admission of children to communion is not to be found consistently across the Anglican Communion. In several provinces, and particularly American experience in the Episcopal Church, practice consistently reflects the theology that baptism is sufficient and children routinely share in the sacrament. If I began with the picture of a child at an English communion rail asking 'Why can't I have some?', then I end this introduction with the picture that has often warmed my heart of the communion rail in an American church with people of every age, from youngest to oldest, stretching out hands to receive, the children with a particular mixture of reverence and eagerness, and even of children distributing the sacrament to adults. Such a picture looks like a window into the feasting of the kingdom of God.

Children and Holy Communion

The story so far

Nick Harding

Issues surrounding the admission of children to communion before confirmation are not new, as Bishop Michael has touched upon in Chapter 1. Here, in this quick dash through the past and current practice on this issue, we will see that the wider Church has held a range of views on the matter.

The early Church

The image we have of the early Church enjoying Holy Communion together is that the sharing of bread and wine was part of a family meal open to all members of the church and their families of all ages. The breaking of bread among believers, as first mentioned in Acts 2.42, makes no distinction between those who are young or older, and no distinction between those who fully understand the significance of the act and those who are simply doing what others do when they gather together. It is understood that the principle of the 'household' gathering would include all family including children, and in addition any other people who were part of the household including servants.

From what we know of worship in the early Church, baptism became the first step in 'membership'. The dramatic and vivid account of Paul and Silas in prison from Acts 16 gives us a clue. After an earthquake Paul and Silas remain in prison despite the possibility of escape, and the jailer and his family are all baptized together as a sign of belief in Jesus Christ. However, we do not know whether baptism was a pre-requisite for joining in with the shared meal of bread and wine or not.

So as Bishop Michael also points out in Chapter 1, the practice of the early Church only partially helps us – there is no explicit mention of any special age-related approach to baptism in the New Testament.

Children were included with the family and household and initiated into the faith with the adults. Nor is there any mention of any baptized or non-baptized members being excluded from the celebration of the Eucharist. The growing tradition seems to have been that for children, as for anyone else, membership of the Church was by baptism and depended on participation in the Eucharist.

The developing Church

As the Church began to grow and spread, so habits developed into traditions, and doctrine also grew to give some direction to the order and form of worship.

Up to the third century it appears that children shared in all rites, and there was no restriction placed on them by age, frequency of worship or level of spiritual understanding. Effectively churches were still in general informal gatherings of believers. However, with the churches in various regions beginning to create leadership structures including bishops, the formalized natures of specific prayers and liturgy was beginning to develop.

Augustine's doctrine of 'original sin'

The concept of original sin was first mentioned in the second century by Irenaeus, Bishop of Lyon. Then later Augustine also developed the doctrine, seeing it as based on the New Testament teaching of Paul the Apostle (Romans 5.12–21 and 1 Corinthians 15.22) and the Old Testament verse of Psalm 51.5. The argument, in simplest form, suggests that all are born sinful and therefore an early rite such as baptism must happen as soon as possible in order to provide a child with any chance of redemption. In practical terms this therefore encouraged the early baptism of infants to secure their future in heaven. Up until this period the bishop was the minister of baptism and the rite included the laying on of hands. As dioceses grew in size, visits from the bishop became infrequent, so local ministers performed the baptism with water and the signing of the cross. The laying on of hands at confirmation came later with the bishop's visit, with potentially the 'confirmation' being more the bishop confirming what was done in his name than the individual confirming the promises made on his or her behalf at baptism. Admission to communion was through baptism as far as we know, and was still open to all ages. During this period baptism, confirmation and communion came to be seen as separate events for a variety of practical reasons including the availability of bishops.

In the eleventh century controversy arose about the way the Church was organized, who had the power and authority to appoint priests and deacons and whether the Church developing in the West based on Rome or the East was the 'true' Church. As the two 'wings' of the Church argued and finally separated, a number of other issues were raised as areas of difference and controversy, including eucharistic presence and the nature of the bread used. A by-product of this was that the Church withheld the bread from children, although it is unclear what a 'child' was considered or defined to be. Later it decided to withhold the cup from all lay people, so children had no way of receiving communion at all. Meanwhile the Eastern Church continued with the practice of early baptism and communion for all.

In 1281 Archbishop Peckham held the Council of Lambeth, a significant event where the rather stern and uncompromising Archbishop of Canterbury produced a number of orders and ecclesiastical laws to reform and tidy up the structures and workings of the Church in England and Wales. Coming from a background as a scholar and monk, he had high expectations of his fellow bishops, priests and even the laity, producing directions on the doctrines and information that priests should be teaching their congregations. It is thought that he didn't understand the pressures that priests faced with more mundane and material matters, and instead expected what we would now call '110 per cent' from them! As part of his reforms he issued a

regulation that those not confirmed – without good reason – should be barred from communion; a new and significant step away from inclusion. It was never clear what 'good reason' could be accepted, so in reality this would have related to children and to adults too, and marked a significant move away from anyone receiving communion before confirmation.

The Reformation

Cranmer's Prayer Book of 1549 stated that 'there shall none be admitted to the Holy Communion until such time as he can say the catechism and be confirmed'. This new directive reaffirmed what had become practice since the Council of Lambeth, further emphasizing the importance of instruction and understanding the faith. From this point a clear connection is made; the consequence of knowledge being personal salvation and commitment. Catechism classes before confirmation were not made available or offered to small children, it being thought that children below an undefined age could not understand the teaching. Thus Anglicans inherited the belief that children could not be admitted to communion until they had been instructed and confirmed.

The twentieth century

The Church of England

Not much appears to have happened to move the issue of children and communion forward until the end of the 1960s, although plenty of anecdotal evidence suggests that some priests were turning a blind eye to the rules and regulations, and practising an 'open table' where all present are welcome to receive both the bread and the wine. Then followed a few decades of slow progress, and experimentation. Some of this has not been helped by priests trying to do what they felt was good by offering children the bread only, or biscuits, or sweets instead of bread as a halfway stage!

As Bishop Michael explains in Chapter 1, in 1969 the **Ely Commission** was asked to reconsider questions of initiation. Its report, *Christian Initiation: Birth and Growth in the Christian Society*,[1] concluded that baptism is complete sacramental initiation and that adults and children should be admitted to Holy

Communion on that basis. Radical and challenging in nature, it took a while for this to be digested and fully understood, and it didn't turn out to be as successful as many would have hoped. The report was referred to dioceses for consideration and debate, and the issue returned to General Synod a few years later.

In 1976 the **General Synod** of the Church of England met and decided not to proceed to a change in the admission of children to communion with a 60:40 majority, notwithstanding the careful and considered findings of the Ely Commission. The issue was 'parked' for a while despite the relatively narrow vote against.

In 1983 a **working party** was commissioned, resulting in the 'Knaresborough Report', *Communion Before Confirmation?*, published in 1985.[2] It recommended the drawing up and approval of regulations for the admission of baptized people to Holy Communion. This was not endorsed by General Synod, but instead a small number of 'experimental' dioceses – Manchester, Peterborough and Southwark – began the practice.

The 1993 **Culham College Institute** report, *Communion before Confirmation*,[3] which looked at what had happened in the three 'experimental' dioceses of Manchester, Peterborough and Southwark, found a substantial majority of the parishes were 'convinced of the positive value of admitting children before confirmation'.

In 1995 the *On the Way* report[4] encouraged parishes to review their patterns of initiation. One of the options was admission of children to communion at an earlier age, while reserving confirmation as a rite of adult commitment.

In March 1997 the House of Bishops issued the 'Guidelines on the Admission of Baptised Persons to Holy Communion before Confirmation', **GS Misc 488**, which had previously been presented to General Synod in July 1996 and approved in November 1996. The **Guidelines** were welcomed by Synod, and an increasing number of dioceses took up the opportunity to offer communion to children before confirmation, even though Canon Law was yet to be changed.

In 2005 the **House of Bishops** debated a proposed change to Canon Law in order to normalize the current process of 'Admission of Baptised Persons to Communion before Confirmation'. Progress was made, and later presented to General Synod.

In February 2006 **new Regulations**, very similar to the previous Guidelines, were approved by General Synod and came into effect on 15 June 2006. These form Canon B15A (see the end of this chapter for a web link).

In July 2011 two **new Eucharistic Prayers** were submitted to General Synod by the Liturgical Commission, after two years' of work and review by the House of Bishops. The two new prayers were subsequently approved and have been widely used since September 2012. They are specifically aimed at being 'suitable for use on occasions when a significant number of children are present or when it is otherwise pastorally appropriate to meet the needs of children present'. The prayers are not as ambitious or creative as some would have liked, but are certainly proving to be popular.

The practice in other Christian Churches

This process in the Church of England is mirrored in many other denominations (Methodist and URC, for example) and in other parts of the Anglican Communion (Canada, New Zealand, Australia and South Africa). Roman Catholic practice is for children to receive their first communion around the age of seven. Eastern Orthodox Churches have always acknowledged the need of children to receive Holy Communion from their baptism, and many would see the Orthodox churches as being closest to original Christian practice.

Many free churches and Baptist churches do not baptize until teenage years or adulthood, and baptism is generally linked with membership of the Church. The whole understanding of baptism is different, and the two traditions cannot realistically be compared.

The situation now

All dioceses in the Church of England welcome children to communion before confirmation, but the 'take up' by parishes varies. It remains the bishop's decision as to whether he or she allows churches to admit children to communion before confirmation, and a bishop could in theory withdraw that permission without affecting those who had already been given permission.

One of the current issues that some churches struggle with is that children who receive communion in their 'home' church should not be refused the sacraments at any other Church of England church. Therefore, visiting children should be offered communion even if the children of that church are not allowed to receive.

The 2006 regulations cover the law and practice in relation to children receiving communion before confirmation. For the full regulations, see <www.churchofengland.org/education/children-young-people/ministry-with-children/children-and-holy-communion.aspx>. Here is a brief summary of the key points of the legislation.

- Children must be baptized, but not ready for or wanting to be confirmed at this point.

- The bishop has the right to allow or revoke permission.

- Incumbents should apply to the bishop in writing, with evidence of a PCC resolution in favour.

- The bishop should only grant permission if he feels sure that it is right to do so.

- Permission for a parish remains in force unless that parish applies for it to be withdrawn.

- The incumbent should be sure that the child has been baptized, and the parents/carers have given permission.

- Children who are admitted should not be refused communion in any other services of Holy Communion conducted according to Church of England rites.

- The rules also apply to cathedrals, with the dean carrying out the incumbent's responsibilities.

- A diocesan bishop can delegate responsibilities to his or her other bishops or archdeacons.

How to take children's admission to communion forward

Every diocese will have different expectations and processes, but each church must make sure that the whole congregation is consulted and has considered the issue well. The PCC must approve the step forward into allowing children to receive communion before confirmation. Some dioceses will have children's advisers who take the lead, while others will work directly with the bishop's office, and have a system managed by the bishop's chaplain. As an example, the process that one diocese operates is shown on page 12 ('Checklist for parishes').

The consultation period with the church is key to a successful process in which the whole community understands the issues and moves forward together. The next chapter, 'Taking the next steps', gives much more advice and support for this process.

Checklist for parishes

This checklist is designed to assist parishes that are considering admitting children to communion before confirmation. Please consider these issues before making an application:

Consultation

- Has the PCC discussed this subject in the light of the Regulations?
- What was the outcome?
- How has the wider congregation been involved in the discussion (including any Local Ecumenical Partnership established under Canon B 44, or other participating churches)?
- What was the outcome?
- What other guidance or advice has been sought (if any)?

Preparation

- How will the preparation of the children for Holy Communion be organized?
- Who will lead the preparation, and what training will they be given?
- What teaching materials will be used?
- How will the children's understanding of communion continue to grow after they have been admitted to Holy Communion?

Pastoral matters

- How will parents be involved in the preparation of their children for Holy Communion?
- What strategy do you have for families who do not wish for their children to be admitted to Holy Communion?
- What strategy do you have for children who come to church without their parents?
- What provision will be made for the nurture of children with learning difficulties who wish to receive Holy Communion?
- How will children be involved and affirmed as members of the Christian communion:
  - within the Eucharist?
  - in non-eucharistic worship?
  - in social events?

Practical arrangements

- Will children be given a Certificate of Admission?
- Who will be responsible for maintaining the register of people admitted to communion before confirmation?

  Note: This register must be kept and made available for inspection.

Help and advice

Advice and help is available from a number of clergy and lay leaders who have taken parishes through this process. The children's adviser, if there is one in the diocese, is also available for consultation and should be referred to during the period of discussion and decision making.

PART

2

Preparing the ground

A case study from a church considering admitting children to Holy Communion

Nick Harding

The following case study is a composite, based on a number of real-life scenarios. Identities have been changed.

St John's is one of three churches looked after by the priest-in-charge, Paul. The other two are tiny communities with very few in the congregations; one is happy to stick to a fortnightly BCP Communion, the other prefers weekly services with communion twice a month and a 'service of the word' led by lay people the other weeks.

St John's is located in a growing commuter village some 20 minutes from a city in the Midlands. It has traditionally been loosely evangelical in nature, serves the predominantly professional class community well and is much respected in the village. The church is blessed with a connected church centre that is widely used by church groups and let to community groups for some regular events.

The congregation of St John's is made up of a full range of ages: there are many older people, many of whom prefer the earlier said communion service. Younger families have moved to the village and are having an impact on church life, as many of them worshipped in churches of other denominations when living closer to the city.

Paul has been incumbent at St John's and the other two churches for three years, having had a previous career as a secondary school teacher. His curacy was in a more traditional and liberal church near the city centre, and throughout his ministry he has shown a particular interest in growing the children, youth and families work that the church does. He has long been aware of the legislation that allows children to receive communion before confirmation, and he has been on a diocese training event on the subject during his curacy. Now he is faced with

dealing with the issue for his own church, as there are children from two families that have moved to St John's who received communion in their previous parishes and expect to be treated the same here. He has already talked with the children and youth team about a unified plan for the development and nurture of children into Christian adults, and he sees children being able to receive communion as a key part of that nurture plan.

The parents from one family said, 'We didn't know there was an issue with this – it's what they do at St Jude's, and we thought it was the same everywhere.'

Paul, working with the wardens and children and youth leaders, decides on his plan of action to raise the issue with the church and the congregation. He knows that there will be a range of views, and in many ways fears the potential for division and disharmony in what is becoming a recognized and growing successful church. He knows he would like the church to accept and approve a motion supporting children receiving communion, but tries to enter the fray as objectively as possible.

Their plan is to raise the subject as a matter of information at the next PCC meeting, and go through a careful process including:

- teaching on Holy Communion in both 'adult' and all-age services;

- discussions with relevant advisers in the diocese, in particular the children's and youth advisers and bishop's chaplain;

- conversations with clergy colleagues from similar churches who have worked through this issue;

- a questionnaire for parents and anyone else interested from the various congregations;

- a PCC meeting to discuss the issue;

- an open meeting principally for parents and carers, with notes to report to PCC;

- PCC resolution – or not – to request permission from the bishop for St John's;

- PCC resolutions for the other two churches in due course.

Paul and one of the two Readers put together two sermons on Holy Communion, and delivered them at all the services on one day in all three churches. For the smaller churches it was less of an issue, and they rarely have children attending. But comments back from these elderly congregations were surprisingly positive.

> We are remembering Jesus' life and celebrating his gift of life to us all – and that includes everyone.

> I don't think I would mind if a child came to the rail and received – it would be a lovely thing to see. We don't get many children in churches these days.

> I wasn't confirmed until my 40s, but took communion since coming back to church when my daughter was born. I didn't know I wasn't allowed, and no one stopped me!

After the services at St John's, and the all-age service the following Sunday, views began to be aired. There were strong views evident, and it took all of Paul's calm and gentle patience to avoid clear groups of 'pro' and 'anti' forming. The questionnaires gave people an opportunity to express what they felt, some with real strength and passion:

> For me one of the important principles is children can make good short-term decisions for themselves, much younger than they can make good long-term or life-changing decisions. To receive communion is a decision I think they can make.

> Some parents just can't accept a change to what was done when they were growing up. It's a difficult thing to change the major landmarks in life. I don't think we should rock the boat.

My grandchildren receive in their own church, and at first I disapproved. But when I visit them now, I love going with them and taking the bread and wine next to them. They really do take it seriously.

> We have to become a more inclusive church, and that has to include children. What's stopping us?

> I had to wait for communion after confirmation, and all of my friends did. If we do this [admit before confirmation] we make it all too cheap and easy.

> In our last church (Baptist) this isn't possible – it's all about understanding. How can children understand what happens at communion? I don't think they can.

> There's a variety of opinion in church. No child has ever mentioned it to me in 11 years of doing children's work, so why go through all this?

> I am uncomfortable with seeing the . . . children receiving, when other children don't. I am worried that we will have two classes of children in our church.

Paul asked one of the children's leaders to do some work collating comments on the questionnaires, and noticed that although there were some strong voices against, most people were either for the idea or in need of more information.

The next PCC meeting looked at the results of the comments and considered the 'rules', including the fact that children have to be baptized first, and they must have some form of preparation. Then they found the discussion spreading to the church's attitude to young people and adults with learning difficulties. Most came to the conclusion that it is difficult to 'test' understanding of what God may be doing through his spirit with those who can't communicate it well. Some saw the connection between those special cases and children (and many adults) in general – can anyone fully understand God and his works in and through us? Paul ended the discussion with an invitation for the PCC to talk more with others in the congregation over the coming weeks, and to come back to the next PCC ready to make a decision.

Although trying hard to remain objective, Paul was directly asked what his views were when popping in to say 'hello' to the Mothers' Union. For a few minutes he spoke to them from the heart about his desire to be an inclusive church, where all people found God in their own ways, at their own level of understanding. He also accepted that some people would struggle with this if the change were to happen, but the overwhelming experience of other churches he had spoken to was that it soon beds down, and families appreciate their children being made to feel much more part of the church. They listened attentively, and at the end of the meeting a few MU members decided to talk to their contacts in other churches too.

Paul had that sinking feeling in the pit of his stomach as the open meeting approached. They had decided to make the event open to anyone from the three churches, and children were able to attend. The chosen time was 4 p.m. on a Sunday, a good time for many people, particularly parents, and a couple of volunteers from a neighbouring parish provided childcare in the church centre. The meeting would be followed by some refreshments, before a short evening service.

The open meeting proved to be a really good time, despite the fact that many opposing views were heard. Most of the traditionalists who wanted things to stay the same because 'that's the way it is' didn't attend, and the main discussion revolved around what people's experiences were in other denominations and whether children who didn't receive would feel different and excluded. Some parents wanted their children to be prepared to receive but didn't want them to have to be baptized first. A few children were there with their parents and were invited to contribute if they wanted to. Some of the opinions voiced were as follows:

> I can't begin to think about allowing my child to receive communion until she has made a life-long commitment to Christ, but I don't want her feeling left out. I feel like I'm being bounced into this decision . . .

> My experience of the Roman Catholic system of first communion is very positive, but I'm struggling with the way it's done in the Church of England!

> I want to do this – I am part of the church too, and I feel left out of something special.

> I guess we (parents) will have to think about our views on baptism again. This raises more issues . . . than we had thought it would.

> I am struggling with this, but now we are part of this church and this is what you do, then my boys can go for it . . . if they want to.

The notes from the open meeting, plus information from other individuals and groups in the church, were brought to the next PCC meeting as planned. As this was the main item for discussion and decision, Paul allowed for a pause for prayer and worship once all the other business was done. In discussion it soon became clear that most of the PCC were willing to step forward and to admit children to communion, with some remaining concerns around the following key questions:

- What age would be the youngest for children to be prepared and admitted?

- Who would be doing the preparation sessions?

- What would they consist of, and would they include parents and carers?

- Who makes the final decision on each child or children?

The age issue proved to be the most contentious. Paul had already ascertained that the diocesan bishop did not set an age, and left it up to each parish. In the end the PCC decided that five would be the very youngest, although some argued for seven and the beginning of Key Stage 2, while others wanted the church to adopt an 'open table' policy and welcome anyone.

The preparation sessions were going to be run by a key children's worker with Paul's assistance, and two sessions for parents would take place. It was also agreed that, unless a child was proving to be particularly immature or flippant about the whole thing in the preparation sessions, then the decision would always rest with the parents or carers.

After the meeting Paul completed the forms the diocese used, and sent the application off to the bishop's office. Within a few days a certificate was received, and in the newsletter as well as from the front Paul invited any parents who wished their children to be prepared to receive communion to have a word with him.

And so the process had begun, and the St John's church moved forward with 12 children in the first group of those wishing to receive. The following year Paul took the proposal to the PCCs of his other two churches, and after seeing first-hand the experience of it at St John's they both approved with little dissent.

Reflections on the case study

There is no model plan for preparing a church or churches for looking at this issue, as each context is unique and needs to be handled in different ways. Nor does the issue sit along party lines of different traditions. For example, there are broadly evangelical churches that struggle on the question of 'understanding', with others from the same tradition wanting the Eucharist to be as open and inclusive as possible. Some at the more catholic end of the church would see 'first communion' as an important marker in the faith development of children, while others would oppose anything that would challenge the place of confirmation at around age eleven. If a church has realistically and purposefully considered how it raises and nurtures children and young people, and decides that this doesn't work in their context, then at least they have thought things through properly.

The key thing that Paul at St John's demonstrates is that it is very important for church members to have the opportunity to discuss the issues, think them through and talk to other churches. Involvement of wider groups in the church such as Mothers' Union, men's groups, teenagers and so on can also help, as everyone then feels some level of 'ownership' of the decision that is finally made. Time needs to be taken over the process, and inevitably some people will continue to have questions and concerns.

Children may or may not have a view on whether they should be allowed to receive the bread and wine. We need to remember that they may not necessarily have the words or confidence to say what they feel, and they may never have considered the issue because this is the way it has always been for them. That doesn't mean that we shouldn't ask them, or ask ourselves what it may feel like for a child to be unable to take part in a key moment in the church's worshipping life. Issues of inclusivity, justice and God's grace all come in to the mix, and as adults we have to try to interpret those and look at them from a child's view.

Each diocese will have advice to offer, and many have a checklist and form for parishes to complete when asking the bishop for permission (see Chapter 2). Members of the congregation and local clergy will have past knowledge and insights to offer. And most of all, experiences of other churches that have started out on this road can prove invaluable.

Taking the next steps
Working with your church and PCC
Nick Harding

Children and communion can be a difficult issue, and not all church members will either understand or support the suggestion. This can be for a number of reasons, from the pastoral to the traditional, with their understanding of 'tradition' stopping at a certain point in history! In the first part of this chapter we will explore some of the common objections and questions that are raised regarding children receiving communion before confirmation. Later in the chapter we will look at how a whole congregation might explore the issue.

First, we'll look at some of the issues and common objections that will be raised.

Common objections and questions

There are some arguments that are very familiar, and come up time and again in churches as they begin to explore this area. Here are some of the most common arguments, and some thoughts as to how to help people explore them more effectively.

'Children can't understand what communion is'

The question of children understanding what communion stands for and represents is often an issue. St Paul talks about recognizing or 'discerning the body of the Lord' (1 Corinthians 11.29) rather than 'understanding' (see Michael Perham's discussion of this issue on page 7), and this was written in the context of the fledgling Church starting to think through what their words and actions actually meant. Young children may not have the vocabulary or formal concepts to express their understanding but yet have a deep appreciation of the significance of the Eucharist. Their formal understanding will grow as they partake alongside their parents and other adults.

Children learn by doing. The adults may well find that their own 'discerning' is deepened as they receive alongside a child, and see that the Holy Spirit moves in all, not just the more mature.

The issue of 'understanding' is often a discussion point in churches where people have come from other church traditions where communion is linked much more strongly with adult membership. Yet if we were to talk individually to adults as they receive the bread and the wine, they would all have a slightly different and more or less developed thinking on what the Eucharist is. If we see faith as more of a mystery, the result of the Holy Spirit moving among God's people, there can be no right or wrong answer.

'There will be noise and disruption during the Eucharist'

Experience shows that this is not normally the case. On the contrary, children who are included are less likely to be disruptive. The presence of children reminds us that the origins of Holy Communion are embedded in the Passover, a family feast in which children play an essential and valued role. They should be welcomed joyfully, and their parents helped to relax.

A church was struggling with this issue, and despite quite a number of people being in favour of moving forward, the PCC vote was closely against. The key argument for many was their perception that children would misbehave at the altar rail. A few weeks after the divisive vote a grandchild came to worship with her grandparents. She was seven, and had been admitted to receive in her own church, so the priest had no alternative but to offer her the bread and wine. The very act of her going forward and taking communion changed the views of some of the previously opposed members of the congregation, as they witnessed a child receiving with due respect for the moment.

'Children don't want or need this change'

It's possible that some groups of children in churches may well be content with the way things are, or it may be that no one has actually asked them. It is difficult for children to know what they are missing if they have never seen or understood that children could receive.

It is not infrequent to find that young children are asking their parents – in their own words – why they cannot share fully in the communion. Their eager eyes look at the priest with expectation, as they expect to be treated the same as all the other people who are kneeling. Sometimes there is a real feeling of rejection that children are suffering in silence. It is important that we engage with the all-age church concept by taking time to ask the children and the parents about their thoughts and feelings.

Children who are offered the opportunity to prepare for and receive communion before confirmation may choose not to. Two boys in one church family were offered the option at the same time, when the church had decided in PCC to move forward on this. The older boy decided this was something he wanted to do, while the younger, who also had a deep understanding of what it was all about, decided that at that stage this was not something for him. There was no jealousy, and no sense of superiority or inferiority – the choice had been offered and the decision had been made by the individuals.

'Confirmation will lose its place in the process'

This is an important issue. The role of confirmation is a topic of debate nationally in the Church and has been for decades. There is a growing sense that as children are admitted to communion, confirmation regains its rightful place as the time when a young person – or adult – makes a public confession of commitment to Christ and his church and receives the confirmation of the Holy Spirit through the laying on of hands of the bishop.

Confirmation has been called 'the rite that is desperately seeking a theology', and it has its own problems that are in no way connected with children receiving communion. Young people tend not to see 'membership' as being hugely significant in the Church and in society generally, and are much more likely to attend and get involved in a church that suits their style rather than choosing by denomination.

At the present time there is real concern that many youngsters are confirmed and then quickly fall away. Anecdotal evidence suggests that children who have been admitted to communion before confirmation are likely to stay in the Church after the move from primary to secondary education (when the Church currently loses 70 per cent of its children), and are more ready to treat confirmation seriously. Whether children are admitted to communion or not, the Church needs to think carefully about how it includes or excludes the young and how it aims to nurture the faith of all believers regardless of their age.

'Children should wait until they are older'

Certainly this is true in some respects. There is real concern that our society forces children to grow up too quickly, and expects mature activities and behaviours too young. The question is, which things should they wait for? Is communion one of them? As a sacrament, Holy Communion is 'a means of grace' that our heavenly Father provides for us. We must ask whether there is any good reason to deny that means of grace to children, perhaps reflecting on the question Jesus asked about an earthly parent giving his child 'a stone when he asked for bread' (some translations of Luke 11.11). Receiving that grace in the Eucharist as part of God's family can help protect our children from the pressures and temptations of the world.

There is also a practical issue here. Children have changed, childhood has changed and the way children learn has changed. Children are much more used to experiential learning than in the past, and like to take part in order to learn more. They are also given some say and control in the institutions, clubs and groups they belong to, and therefore feel they have a stake in the organization. If church is the one place where children are not allowed some involvement and participation, they will not feel it is 'theirs' and will make the subconscious decision to leave it behind, sooner or later.

'I had to wait – today's children should too'

This is an understandable view, one often raised by older members of the congregation. If we take a step back we shall recognize that during the past half century the Church has lost the great majority of two generations. The middle-aged among us who have remained faithful are the exception, not the rule. There are many factors contributing to this, but we must ask ourselves what part was played by the Church's attitude to children. Perhaps the question for people who have that view would be, 'Where are all your peers who went to church now?', and 'Would your peers still be worshipping if they had been more valued when you and they were younger?' One head teacher said recently, when discussing churchgoing as a child, 'I was in church three times every Sunday singing in the choir. But no one ever took a scrap of interest in me as an individual.' This man became an avowed atheist and his views influenced thousands of children throughout his career. We should try to avoid the tragic mistakes of the past, and think through what it really means to include children in the worshipping life of our church communities.

'There is no need for preparation'

This is an understandable reaction from those who think we should follow the Orthodox pattern of welcoming all, whatever their age. It resonates in that, by working through some sort of preparation course, we are moving towards children being expected to 'understand', when we can just as easily argue that it is not about understanding but God's grace. Making children prepare may also reinforce the discriminatory aspect of assessing spirituality due only to age. Most churches don't, for instance, ask adults what their understanding is of communion or insist that they attend a course before receiving regularly. Many regular communicant adults may have received instruction before confirmation but many may not have even been confirmed.

The requirement that children who wish to be active partakers in the feast are prepared for this is seen by some as a bit of an 'Anglican fudge' – a halfway house that is not at one extreme or the other. But on the positive side, if children go through a preparation course it is a means of reinforcing the significance of receiving the bread and wine, the elements of communion, and helps children think through their own faith at their own level. In reality it may mean that children who receive at the Eucharist have a better knowledge than many adults, and therefore have something valuable to teach the more mature worshippers around them.

'A child may be turned away when in another church'

The regulations state that if a child receives at their own church they should not be excluded from communion at a church where they are a visitor, whether that church allows its own children to receive or not. As we have seen earlier, this can have advantages in children modelling what actually happens when they receive – showing that there's no thunderbolt from heaven and chaos does not ensue!

Children should not be turned away, although this has sometimes happened. In some cases it could simply be that the priest was unaware that the child is a regular communicant in their home church, but sadly there have been cases where priests have refused solely on their own grounds. This is in opposition to Canon Law, and therefore could result in some form of censure.

'We don't have children in our church, so there's no point considering this'

Such churches may be a small community, perhaps in a rural area with few or no regular children. The important thing is to be prepared for that moment when, perhaps unexpectedly, a family walks through the door. A bishop tells the story of earlier in his ministry when he moved to such a church, and as well as encouraging the church to pray for children he also asked two members of the church to prepare materials should any children appear. It took some months, but eventually and slowly children and families started to attend, and the church was not only delighted at the answer to prayer, they were also ready for them.

A church that is ready and welcoming is far more likely to keep that family than one that is not. Considering the question of admitting children to communion is part of the process of getting ready, aiming to be a church that wants to be in a position to welcome and value children, young people and families. The 2014 Church of England report into church growth, *From Anecdote to Evidence*,[1] highlights that churches that grow are ones that welcome and include children and families.

'This could be divisive, so we're avoiding it'

This is one of a number of pastoral issues that may be raised. The bottom line for the Church of England is that 'Baptism always precedes admission to Holy Communion' (House of Bishops Guidelines 1997). In such situations, great sensitivity will be needed for the church to move forward together, whichever way the decision on admitting children to communion goes. This can also be an issue to be worked through when churches are in ecumenical agreements and partnerships, and the current practice of the other denomination or minister differs from our regulations.

There will need to be time for honest discussion, for empathy and for much prayer. There is certainly some value in a church community sitting down and thinking through what it understands as initiation, membership and inclusion. The experience of other parishes that have faced similar issues may be helpful, and each diocese will know who could offer support in the more difficult of these situations. Many of these issues appear when members of the congregation are from other church traditions, and have not fully understood or are unable to accept the meaning of baptism and communion within the Church of England.

'Parents/carers may not understand what the children are doing.'

This is another important pastoral issue, and each individual case may need careful consideration. In some cases the 'responsible adult' in church is a grandparent or a friend's parents, and their role could be vital in helping the child develop in his or her faith. All children need 'significant adults' in their lives and in their spiritual lives too. Many of the published courses of preparation for communion either involve parents – as does our course in Chapter 6, 'Feasting together' – or include at least one session for parents or other responsible adults who will be supporting the child through this process. There is real value in sitting down with

parents or adult carers during the preparation process and helping them understand what the children are doing in the context of their own faith journey. For those who are regular worshippers, this will challenge them to consider their own faith journey, and for those who are on the fringe of church or not involved at all, it may spark something spiritual inside them that could even lead to those adults wanting to find out more themselves, and stepping forward into communion or confirmation.

Working with the whole church to explore the issue

Children and communion should always been seen in the context of the Church's commitment to faith development and nurture across the generations, and not in isolation. If churches take this seriously there could be a number of steps to go through, and wider issues to be grappled with.

Sermons and other teaching

As this is a significant step in the life of the church, the church and its congregation or congregations should all have an opportunity to think and to learn about the Eucharist and children. This teaching and exploration could be done through sermons, talks or smaller group sessions.

Bible passages to discuss

There are a number of short Bible passages that may be of assistance when thinking through the issues. For each there are a few questions to consider, and some background notes for a leader if these were used in a discussion group.

1 *The Last Supper: Matthew 26.17–30*

   Suggested questions

   - Who were the people Jesus was eating with?

   - Did they expect this meal to have special significance?

   - Why were children and women not there?

   - Is the gift of sharing bread and wine for certain people only?

   Leaders' notes

   Jesus was with his closest team of male disciples, as would have been culturally normal at the time. But that isn't to say that the model of sharing bread and wine was only appropriate to adult male followers of Christ. The gift is offered to all the disciples despite their frailty and weaknesses, of which Jesus was fully aware. They are likely to have struggled to understand what Jesus was saying and explaining, yet still he offered and still they received. The gift seems to be for all people.

2 Children recognize Jesus: Matthew 21.12–16

Suggested questions

- Why was Jesus distressed at how the temple was being used?

- Who did he decide to help?

- Who recognized who Jesus was, and shouted it out?

- What was his response to the chief priests and teachers of the law?

- What can we learn about children from this?

Leaders' notes

Jesus was distressed at how the temple was being misused, and quickly turned it back to a place of God, healing those who came to him. Meanwhile children were shouting out 'Hosanna to the son of David', having recognized not just who Jesus was, but what Jesus was. The 'religious' had failed to see this, but children and their open spirituality were led by God to speak out what they knew. Children are spiritual beings, they are open to God.

3 Jesus welcomes children: Mark 10.13–16

Suggested questions

- Why did people want Jesus to bless their children?

- Do you think the disciples were surprised to be rebuked?

- Was Jesus' welcome to these children partial or conditional?

- Would Jesus have denied these children what they needed?

- What does it mean to obstruct children coming to Jesus?

Leaders' notes

This and the other similar Gospel passages clearly suggest that Jesus wants to fully welcome children. The disciples may have been surprised as at the time it would have been countercultural and exceptional to focus on children in this way. Jesus warns against hindering children on their faith journey or stopping them coming to him. Sometimes the Church could be accused of this – we are inclined to be exclusive rather than inclusive, and put rules and regulations in the way of children coming to Jesus.

4 Parents and children's spirituality: 1 Corinthians 7.14

Suggested questions

- What does this verse say about parents' spiritual responsibility?

- Are children 'spiritual beings'?

- Can children be called 'unworthy' based on this passage?

Leaders' notes

This verse gives us a clue as to the spirituality of children. It suggests that if a parent or carer has faith, children also share that faith. This is demonstrated in the account of Paul and Silas in prison assisting as the jailor and all of his family become believers (Acts 16.34). Therefore it is difficult to see children as somehow defiled or not worthy of sharing in the eucharistic meal.

5 Communion in the Early Church: 1 Corinthians 11.17–32

Suggested questions

- Why did Paul write this passage?

- Who would have been in the church family?

- Is it clear that this is for adults only?

- Do the warnings of eating without recognizing the body justify excluding some?

- Can children be classed as 'unworthy' in this context?

Leaders' notes

These instructions were written to bring order to the church in Corinth, which appears to be falling short of the expected standards when meeting together.

This indicates that families were coming to worship together, and therefore despite no specific mention of children it can be assumed that they would have been there. There are warnings about being unworthy to receive, but these apply equally, if not more, to adults who have more understanding and are wilfully receiving the bread and wine.

Exploring the meaning of communion with the whole church family

Communion is a celebration that has a number of meanings and implications. These suggestions could be explored with the whole church family, as seems fit.

Giving thanks

As we receive the bread and wine we give thanks for God's gifts to all people, and to us. The gift of Jesus, remembered in the body and blood, is the gift for all people of all ages. We are fed by God in the bread and wine as well as in the word and through prayer.

Remembering God's faithfulness

The Eucharist is the culmination of the journey of God's people to the time of Jesus, including all the challenges of the Old Testament. Through the New Testament stories of Jesus' life and teachings, we remember God's constant love towards all God's people.

Remembering Jesus

The liturgy takes us directly to the moment when Jesus and his disciples shared that last meal together. We are transported to that moment as we receive, and children are just as good – if not better – than many adults in seeing themselves in that picture.

Belonging

Communion is a sign of belonging that makes real the promises of baptism. As we all receive together we are levelled – we are all the same. The boundaries and fences we put up around us are taken away, we are all sinners and we are all forgiven, and all become children of God in his family and sharing in his meal.

Celebration

We celebrate our community of all ages and the presence of God with us as we receive the bread and wine. This celebration is about everything we are and everything that God is to us. That's a lot to celebrate!

The importance of meals

In the Old Testament it is clear from tradition and teaching that meals and feasts are important and carry huge significance. In the Gospels there are a number of meals where Jesus ate with others. Each of these has significance, and may help in thinking through with the whole congregation the significance of the Last Supper.

Feeding of the five thousand: John 6.5–14

Jesus and the disciples are aware of a large crowd who have been gathering and listening to Jesus as he shared wisdom and teaching. The disciples were perplexed as to how they would feed such a crowd, but Jesus used the opportunity to reveal a little of his power, and highlight the gifts that the young can offer. Andrew found a boy who was willing to offer his lunch to be shared, and Jesus performed that much celebrated miracle with that bread and fish.

Points to consider:

- Everyone gathered to eat together from a range of backgrounds and ages.
- Jesus was present at the meal and moved in power.
- A child was willing to offer what he had, and set the adults an example.

The road to Emmaus: Luke 24.25–32

This remarkable account shows us two people who are confused and bewildered by the death of Jesus, and despite the rumours of his resurrection decide to set off straight away from Jerusalem towards Emmaus. In their confusion and lack of understanding Jesus comes alongside them and walks with them. It is only when they stop for food and he breaks bread in the familiar way that he had at the Last Supper that the two realize who it is that has been helping them.

Points to consider:

- We are all on a journey, whatever our age.
- We all have more to learn.
- Jesus comes alongside us and teaches us more – if we are willing to listen.
- Jesus makes himself known to us at the meal.

The meal at the home of Simon the Pharisee: Luke 7.36–47

Simon is important, and as a Pharisee he is taking a bit of a risk offering Jesus hospitality. While they were there eating, a woman known to be sinful came in and washed Jesus' feet with her tears. Then she poured perfume on him. Simon saw this and was confused as to why Jesus would let a woman, and particularly a woman who had sinned as this woman had, do such things to him. Jesus takes the opportunity to speak to Simon and the others present about what forgiveness really is.

Points to consider:

- Meals are special times when Jesus does things!

- Jesus was willing to welcome anyone.

- Jesus broke the traditions and cultures of the time by welcoming a woman.

- Forgiveness is available to all.

The meal on the beach: John 21.1–13

Jesus appears to some of his disciples, who are out on their fishing boats and have not had a successful night. Jesus, on the shore, calls to them and advises them to put their nets out of the other side of the boat. They net a large number of fish, and after Peter has recognized Jesus and has jumped into the water to get to him quicker, they share a meal of bread and fish on the shoreline.

Points to consider:

- Jesus is with us.

- Jesus knows what is best for us to do.

- They recognize Jesus and want to be with him.

- Jesus breaks bread and shares a meal with them all.

Justice issues

We have already looked at how Jesus encouraged people to allow children to come to him. This is for many an issue of justice. Here are some passages that help us consider justice.

Psalm 33.5

It is clear that God is full of both justice and mercy and his word is true. He leads his people throughout the Old Testament with a balance of both, and calls all people to follow his example of justice and to see and share his love for all people over all time.

Proverbs 29.7

Here the people are called specifically to show justice for the 'poor'. It is possible to consider children as equivalents to the poor because of their lack of power and their inability to make decisions alone to determine their own futures. Like our calling to offer the poor justice, so too we must make sure that children are treated fairly and not excluded.

Isaiah 42.1–4

In his prophecy Isaiah describes Jesus, the Messiah. He will be strong and firm, yet gentle and quiet too. He will be filled with the Holy Spirit and he will establish justice on earth. This passage, mirrored later in Matthew 12, reminds us that all that Jesus did was for the good of others, including showing and bringing justice to children.

Activities

Some people prefer to read up on an issue before they are able to engage in the debate. You can photocopy and distribute the leaflet entitled 'Children and communion' on page 29, if it is appropriate for your church situation.

A discussion activity with adults

This activity could be done with PCC or other groups. Sheet 4.1 on page 30 offers some 'Statements for a discussion activity with adults' that you can photocopy, cut up and gather into sets, allowing one set for each group of adults. Each group's task is to prioritize the statements from 'important' to 'unimportant'. Much of the value of this activity is in the discussion and feedback, which needs to be led carefully with sensitive and gentle challenging of inappropriate views and attitudes. This could work in some circumstances as an all-age activity, assuming that the adults allow the children to have their say and make their contribution.

A discussion activity with children and young people

Some children and young people may never have thought through their own faith journey or really considered what communion and confirmation are. Sheet 4.2 on page 31 offers some 'Questions for a discussion activity with children and young people' that you can photocopy and cut up to distribute. With small groups, ask the questions to gauge what the level of understanding is, and try to give some explanations as you go along.

Watching

Some children may not have any idea what happens at communion – they have yet to be included and so don't pay much attention! This 'mystery' can lead to confusion and fear rather than happiness at the prospect of being able to take part. However, in order not to single children out, the priest can invite anyone who wishes – children, young people, adults – to stand to one side of the altar to watch what he or she is doing. Try to avoid this just being children, as adults may be needed to keep an eye on them. Some adults may enjoy the opportunity to do this, and to see the elements at close quarters.

Working through the words

One of the unexpected positive consequences of discussing children being welcomed at the Eucharist is that adults as well as the young have the opportunity to learn more and refresh their own understanding of what communion is. During the period when the issues are being discussed, take one of the words or phrases during a service when all ages are present and very briefly explain what it means. Sheet 4.3 on page 32 offers a simple definition for each, but it is entirely appropriate to add other words and phrases and more information for each. You can photocopy and cut out the words or phrases and their definitions to distribute them in the congregation.

Help and advice

When looking at these complex and significant changes in church practice and patterns of nurture, it is right to get as much help as possible from those outside the context who have understanding and experience to share.

Diocesan Advisers

There will be people at the central level in the diocese who have some responsibility and experience to offer. The bishop's office may administer the process and have some insights. Most dioceses have some level of children and youth adviser support, and they are likely to be able to bring to your PCC the experiences, positives and pitfalls from other places.

Other church leaders

Locally there will be other similar churches that have been through the process. It may be helpful to invite a leader from another church to talk through their experiences, and allay some of the fears members of the PCC and church may have.

Children and young people

There may be children and young people within your congregation who have already received in their previous churches and have things to share. Alternatively, some young people from other churches may be willing to come along to yours and talk about their experience of the preparation course and what it means to them to receive communion.

Parents

Again, you may need to approach other churches to request a few parents to come to PCC or an open meeting and talk through what it meant to them, how they came to a decision for their own children, and the difference it makes to their family.

Children and communion

The history

It is thought that until AD 1200, all ages received communion as a matter of course during worship, and baptism and confirmation happened at the same time. In the twelfth century there was controversy within the Church – the bread was withheld from children and wine from all laity. Orthodox churches continued to offer bread and wine to all ages, as they do today, while later the Protestant Church excluded children on the basis of their perceived level of 'understanding'.

Now in the Church of England

Each diocese may offer the option of children receiving communion before confirmation to churches, and churches are encouraged to consider the issue. Dioceses have guidelines for churches to follow in order to ensure that decisions are properly considered and due care is taken in communion preparation.

Now in other Christian churches

Some other denominations see receiving communion as the norm for all who believe, however young they are and without specific preparation. Others place admission to Holy Communion alongside 'adult' baptism and church membership at a much later stage.

Arguments used in support of admitting children to communion before confirmation

- The whole family of the church worship and receive together, with children learning to behave appropriately.

- Children are welcomed and valued equally, not excluded from a key element of worship.

- Children from other churches are welcomed and children from the church would fit in elsewhere.

- This is the true historical tradition of the Church.

- Children gain specific teaching at a receptive age and understand what they are doing to their level of understanding.

- Confirmation is not rushed into and is therefore enhanced with more appropriate teaching at a suitable age.

Sheet 4.1: Statements for a discussion activity with adults (see page 27)

Photocopy and cut out the separate strips below.

The whole church family should be valued equally

Children should be seen and not heard

Communion/Eucharist is an important service

Communion/Eucharist is for the whole church family

This church is good at welcoming children

Older people should be encouraged to welcome children

Children and families disturb older worshippers

Older adults disturb children and families

All people who receive communion should be confirmed

All people should be allowed to receive communion

Children are open to God and have spiritual lives

Jesus encouraged all people to help children meet him

Sheet 4.2: Questions for a discussion activity with children and young people (see page 28)

Photocopy and cut out the separate boxes below.

How do you feel treated in church?

Does this church value and welcome children and young people?

Is communion a special meal that is only for adults or old people?

Can communion be received only after confirmation?

What happens at Holy Communion?

Sheet 4.3: Simple definitions (see page 28)

Photocopy and cut out the separate boxes below.

Eucharist

The Christian service, ceremony, or sacrament commemorating the Last Supper, in which bread and wine are consecrated and consumed. Based on the Greek for 'thanksgiving'.

Holy Communion

The same as the Eucharist – an opportunity to remember Jesus by the sharing of the bread and wine. In more Catholic gatherings the term 'Mass' may be used.

Last Supper

The name for Jesus' final meal with his disciples (for example, Matthew 26.17–30) where he demonstrated the breaking of bread and sharing of wine.

Bread

This represents Jesus' body, and as he broke it he told his friends that his body would also be broken.

Wine

This reminds us of Jesus' blood, and he shared it, asking his friends to remember that his blood would be shed.

Chalice

This is a cup that the wine is shared from. It is likely that Jesus used a pottery cup, but we can't be sure.

Paten

A plate that is used for the bread at communion.

Remembering

Jesus said to his disciples 'Do this in remembrance of me' (Luke 22.19), asking them to remember him when they share the bread and wine.

PART

3

Preparing the people

A 'getting ready' story
Preparing children for communion before confirmation
Sandra Millar

Note: Although the following story is based on a number of real-life conversations and situations, identities have been changed.

It's Sunday afternoon in a quiet village in the Midlands. But from inside the church comes the sound of chatter and laughter as nine children and fifteen adults come together to explore what it means to receive Holy Communion, using the resources outlined in this book. There are five different families represented, some mums, some dads and a few adults who have come along from the regular worshipping congregation.

There is a level of uncertainty – except from the children, who are enjoying moving around the familiar space at an unfamiliar time. The parents chat to those they recognize, reluctantly sitting at the front where the younger children have congregated. The other adults hang back, perhaps with an air of suspicion, as they want to check out this strange new world of admitting children to communion before confirmation.

The recent decision of the PCC has been followed by permission from the bishop, so the parish is ready to go ahead and prepare a group of children aged from four to twelve years old. Looking back on the experience, one of the mums says: 'I didn't really know what to expect. But the vicar wanted us to come as a family. I was relieved to discover some other mums that I know already were there.'[1]

Most of the parents were there because the vicar told them to come with their children, and to begin with had little expectation of getting anything from it themselves. Some of them recall feeling a bit irritated with having to come along: 'I thought I'd just be able to drop off the kids, then go back home and get on with some work. I mean, I've been receiving communion since I was a teenager, so, yeah, I guess I was a bit grumpy to begin with.'

The adults who came without children came with questions: 'I was one of those who wasn't sure at all when we voted to pass this. I wanted to come along and see how these children behaved, how much they understand, what is going on.'

But others came ready to be supportive: 'I think this is exciting – I hope it will be the start of something new for children in this village and in this church. But I hope I don't have to do anything too hard this afternoon! I can't remember much about my own confirmation.'

This sense of apprehension was common for most of the adults. They weren't given too much information – simply the date, place and length of the two sessions. Some were worried they were already supposed to know things and might be put on the spot, while others were anxious about having to join in with things. Some thought they would just sit at the back and wait.

The children felt differently:

> It's cool being in church when there's nothing happening. We can run about and talk.

> Sunday afternoon is boring anyway – my dad falls asleep in front of the telly, and my mum talks on the phone all the time. I'm not allowed out to play on my own. So this is good.

The children all know one another from the local church school and there are groups of siblings as well. One of the older girls quickly makes a pet out of the four-year-old – who is well able to take care of herself.

They are all encouraged to make name badges for themselves as everyone gathers – even the adults. There is much embarrassed laughter from the adults at first, disclaimers about their ability to draw or write, but the children offer encouragement to their own parents: 'It seemed a bit odd asking all of us to do something, but it was also fun after a bit. I hadn't done any colouring for years.'

One or two of the adults clearly take part with reluctance: 'I thought I'd come to watch,' recalls one member of the congregation, 'so I couldn't see why I needed a badge. But I did it.'

When the formal programme started, there was still a lot of separation between the different groups, even though everyone was being encouraged to speak to everyone else. The adults without children found it the most difficult.

> I felt a bit odd trying to ask children questions. Some of them looked at me as if I was peculiar or something.

But with encouragement the group began to shift, especially as people discovered they had things in common with others from different generations and from different families. Some of the children were amazed to discover that the old man (about 60!) had gone to the same school as them – although a few years earlier.

By the next activity the whole gathering was divided into teams, mixing adults and children together. A competitive task helped to break down barriers further and people of all ages began to work together: 'It was really funny when we all had to get down on the floor to do the puzzle. Mr X was brilliant!' And one of the parents recalls: 'I'd never really had a chance to know X. I thought she was like a good person who went to church and did good things for people. But when we were in the team, helping one another, and helping the children, she turned out to be a real laugh!'

Breaking down barriers and creating a sense of family is one of the key reasons for doing family-based preparation for children to receive communion before confirmation. It emphasizes that church is truly about everyone, and encourages listening and learning from one another. Some time later one of the parents reflects: 'It was different afterwards when we went to church. I felt that I knew people more – and

could be relaxed in church. It was like one of those family Christmas parties – but without the rows!'

As the session continues adults and children began to merge as one group. Adults began to grow in confidence and volunteered to join in. One mum offered to tell a Bible story. Afterwards she said: 'I didn't even know I knew that story! I can't believe I got up the front and told it to everyone.'

The final activity of the first afternoon was about remembering, and triggered an avalanche of cross-generational reminiscing about pets, Christmas, school dinners – everyone seemed to have a story to tell. This was the section that led to thinking about what it means to remember Jesus – to remember everything he did and everything he means. This had a big impact on some of the adults: 'It really made me think again about what communion meant to me. I mean, you just go every week, take the bread, and then go back to your seat. I was really thinking about Jesus and what happened to him, like I haven't for ages.'

By the time everyone shared tea together there was a real family atmosphere, and everyone was looking forward to the second session, just a week later. One of the children said: 'I wish church was always like this!'

The building of relationships across generations and between different groups of people continued at the second session, the following week. During this session the teaching began to focus more deeply on what it means to take communion, although there were also some practicalities that people enjoyed. The adults who were there without children were both moved and challenged by the responses of the children, especially the younger ones: 'I know I thought this was the right thing to do, but I didn't realize how seriously they would take it. I mean, little X, she was amazing. Her face was so serious, and when she talked about Jesus dying as the saddest and most special thing ever, I nearly cried. It made me think.'

The children themselves are more matter-of-fact about the experience:

> I liked it when we learned what all the things were called, 'cos I like knowing the right things. But I liked it too when she told us about Jesus and the bread.

It's weird to think that we are doing the same things as people have done here for ages and ages. Sometimes that gives me a funny feeling when I'm in church waiting to take communion. It's like ghosts but not really.

As with the first session, the programme was interactive and participative, and this time both adults and children were ready to join in. The vicar recalls the way that people listened and learned from one another: 'When it was time to ask questions it was a level playing field. The children asked some simple but profound questions, and the adults asked for practical explanations, but they all listened to the answers. It was just lovely.'

For this small country parish, preparing children to receive communion before confirmation turned out to be as much about building relationships with one another as it was about children knowing the right things. It was also about adults rekindling their own connection with the Eucharist, as they were encouraged to think more deeply. Some of them enjoyed rediscovering things they had learned years ago in confirmation classes, while others found themselves challenged to approach Holy Communion with fresh meaning.

> It must be 40 years since I was confirmed. I'd forgotten all those things about what plates are called, and the little napkin things, and why we do things in a certain way. I liked discovering it again – I remembered how special it was when I was a teenager, and I feel a bit sad that it all gets so ordinary over the years, sort of taken for granted.

One parent found the whole experience challenged the family's faith:

> We came back and our youngest started asking to pray before bedtime, then he began to question some of the things we said over meals. It was like having a living conscience in the house! But it did make me think. I mean communion is more than Sunday, isn't it? [laughs] Don't know how long it'll last! Perhaps we need to do this kind of thing every year or so.

As the months went by, the memories of the experience inevitably faded. However, the people of the parish are sure that they made the right

decision and are looking forward to the next opportunity to work with a group of children exploring communion.

The decision made by the PCC is to admit children to communion before confirmation, and initially parishes might expect that preparing will be about a small group of children gathering for 'lessons' with the vicar. This is partly because they have little experience to draw on except their own memories of confirmation classes, and sessions in the vicar's study or in the church. But preparing children to receive communion before confirmation is not the same as confirmation itself, and should be clearly different in content and style. The focus is wholly about the Eucharist itself, and many of the excellent preparation courses around use the shape and structure of the eucharistic service to shape the programme.

The discussions during the decision-making process will have focused on the sense that Holy Communion is a gift from God, and that we do not receive it because we are good or clever, nor because we understand. It is a mysterious sacrament of God's grace – unconditional love – given to everyone. However, sometimes the demands of a preparation course can seem contrary to this theology, as parents struggle to find a way of committing their child to a course lasting almost three months. For both pragmatic and theological reasons a shorter, more intense programme can be very effective.

Holy Communion is also something that we share together as the body of Christ, mostly when a group are gathered in one place. But even when two are three are gathered there is a sense that we are all connected to the wider Church throughout the world and throughout time. It makes sense, then, to spend some time getting ready to take communion as the people of God, rather than separating the children from their family, whether domestic or congregational. The experience of the congregation above, who were piloting the programme that follows, shows the unexpected benefits of shared learning. Relationships were created and strengthened, and when the children began to share communion regularly on Sundays it really began to feel like a household of faith coming together to share a feast. Alongside these deeper reasons, practically it is a lot easier to bring families together for two Sunday afternoons, which include sharing some food together, than trying to get a family to commit to bringing children for six or more consecutive meetings!

The whole process of admitting children to communion before confirmation can be emotional, sometimes confrontational. But once the children begin to explore what communion means, the parish can begin to move forward with joy, laying aside questions and anxieties, and committing to supporting the families involved. They can be invited along to the sessions, and also encouraged to pray for those involved. The time of preparing can become a time of growth for the whole church.

Feasting together

A family programme to help children get ready for Holy Communion

Sandra Millar

Introduction

This programme has been designed for families to do together, although all the activities would work with a group of children, led by adults. However, as the story revealed, exploring together is a powerful experience.

The simplest way to offer this programme is over two afternoon sessions of about two hours in length, plus time to share hospitality together. This might be as basic as tea and biscuits or sharing a meal together. This is important as it helps to build friendships through the group and strengthens the sense of being included. The programme is presented as two main sessions with a series of activities, but it is possible to split these differently according to your local circumstances.

Who to lead?

It is important that the clergy are present for at least some of the time, but the activities can be led by a group of lay or ordained people who regularly interact with children and families, but are also visibly part of the celebration of communion. This might mean chalice assistants, readers, intercessors, sidespeople or regular members of the congregation. Exploring what it means to take communion is not just about teaching given in words, but it

is also about engaging in the experience of church – discovering what it means to belong, and discovering that the job of celebrating communion is the work of all the people who are gathered.

Where to hold it?

This programme works well in the church itself if that is practical (for example, if the church building is heated or has toilet facilities). Even if a local hall is more suitable for most of the programme, it is important that everyone visits the church at some point and begins to look at the building and the special things used for communion with fresh eyes.

What happens?

The programme is designed to happen over two sessions. Each session contains a number of activities for everyone to do together, and some *Connection* sections that help the presenter of the activity to focus comments towards the Eucharist and the communion service. The plan has been developed to ensure that the central ideas of celebrating and remembering are present in both sessions. However, there is no reason why the programme shouldn't be delivered differently, depending on local traditions.

The Programme

Although two hours is suggested for each session, the actual time may depend on the age and number of people taking part. Generally, the higher the numbers, the longer activities will take. However, if the group is small, more time can be taken for talking and listening to each other. Times next to activities are given for guidance only. Timings allow for regrouping between activities and a short break if needed.

Session 1

- Activity 1: 20 minutes (including gathering time)
- Activity 2: 15 minutes
- Activity 3: 20 minutes
- Activity 4: 15 minutes
- Activity 5: 15 minutes
- Activity 6: 20 minutes
- Allow 5–10 minutes to bring the session to a close and give practical notices.

Session 2

- Activity 1: 10 minutes (including gathering time)
- Activity 2: 10 minutes
- Activity 3: 10 minutes
- Activity 4: 10 minutes
- Activity 5: 20 minutes
- Activity 6: 30 minutes (NB: you may need to allow time to move the group to a different location)
- Activity 7: 10 minutes
- Activity 8: 10 minutes
- Allow 5 minutes to bring the programme to a close.

Session 1 (2 hours)

Activity 1

For this opening activity you will need:
- enough copies for everyone of photocopiable Sheet 6.1, 'Getting to know you', on page 52 (adapted for your situation);
- pens.

DIOCESE OF CHICHESTER

TO KNOW · LOVE · FOLLOW JESUS

Prayer of St Richard

O God of grace and new life,
we pray for your diocese of Chichester;
that in times of challenge and change,
your people may grow in holiness,
and discern your calling to each and to all.
Equip and enable us
in witnessing to Christ,
working for the common good,
and transforming our parishes
in the service of your kingdom;
through Jesus Christ our Lord.

The prayer of St. Richard.
Thanks be to you, our Lord Jesus Christ,
for all the benefits which you have given us,
for all the pains and insults
which you have borne for us.
Most merciful Redeemer, Friend and Brother,
may we know you more clearly,
love you more dearly,
and follow you more nearly,
day by day.
Amen.

 /DioceseofChichester

 @ChichesterDio

 chichester.anglican.org

May God the Father,
your creator, give you life in
abundance and perfection.

May God the Son, Jesus Christ,
show you the path of truth
and reconciliation.

May God the Holy Spirit,
inspire you to live
in faith, hope and love.

Amen

This opening activity is designed to begin the process of breaking down barriers and helping people to get to know each other a little. Although children may know one another well, especially if they go to the same school, parents may not. Other adults from the church may be total strangers to the children and families – although if the church operates a programme like 'Open the Book' (for more information see <www.openthebook.net>), then inviting some of those volunteers along can be a good bridge builder.

Adapt the chart: You will need to use local knowledge to make sure that there are likely to be some people able to tick at least one of the boxes. It's also a good idea to have one thing that only two or three people will have done, and it's also important to make sure that the ideas apply to adults and children – for example, 'Have lived in the same house since I was a baby' can reveal that a nine-year-old and a seventy-year-old have something in common.

Hand out the chart to each person: if there are early readers present, make sure someone is giving them a hand. Explain that everyone is going to walk around and talk to everyone else, trying to get a different signature in each box. The game ends when someone has a signature in every box. (A variation on this is to suggest that they get as many signatures as they can in each box within a time limit. The game ends when the time is up.)

Invite everyone to sit down and then go through some of the answers. Identify any similarities or unusual things people have in common. Bring out the idea of diversity.

Connection: talk about how the church is made up of lots of individuals, each with their own unique story to share. Explain how church is made up of people who gather together to make one community in one space at one time, for example on Sunday morning.

Talk about how we know when it's time for something to begin. Get suggestions from the group either by asking an open question or specifics such as 'How do you know when it's time to stop playing and go into school?' 'How do you know when a football match is due to begin?' 'At the theatre or film, how do you know when to stop talking?'

Explain how your church service usually begins and then introduce the opening words and reply:

Leader The Lord be with you.
All   **And also with you.**

Practise learning those words and repeat them every so often during the session.

Activity 2

In the right order
You will need:

- two (or more) sets of eight cards with the following words individually written on (these are available on photocopiable Sheet 6.2, 'In the right order', on page 53):

  - heat oven

  - weigh ingredients

  - melt butter in saucepan

  - stir in oats

- put in tray

- cook in oven

- cool and divide up

- eat.

Split the group into two mixed-age teams (you will need one set of cards for each team).

Hand each group a set of mixed-up cards. It's a race to see which team can sort them into the right order and work out the recipe (it's for flapjacks).

Ask the congregation to return to their seats.

Connection: talk about the idea of sequence and order. You can't stir in oats until you have weighed the ingredients. Explain that the communion service is the same. It happens in an order that is always the same. Invite the children to try and name some of the parts of the service, if they are already familiar with it. However, take care not to make them feel stupid or inadequate if they don't know or suggest something very different.

The shape of the service

You will need:

- two large card circles (say up to about 28 cm in diameter):

  - one whole;

  - one cut into quarters, labelled 'gather', 'listen', 'celebrate' and 'go out' (see the photocopiable Sheets 6.3 and 6.4, 'The shape of the service A', 'The shape of the service B', on pages 54 and 55).

Assemble the four quarters on to the whole circle, talking about the shape of the communion service as you go.

Before moving to Activity 3, recap Activity 1 to remind everyone of how we gather as God's people and join together by sharing in words and music. (If you wish, this could be a good place to talk about favourite hymns, even sing a verse or two.)

Activity 3

Story time (we listen)

You will need:

- a stopwatch;

- a list of 15 names from the Bible (e.g. Noah, Rachel, Eve, David, Joshua, Nathan, Ruth, Matthew, Joanna, Paul, Martha, Mary, Timothy, John);

- two long strips of paper and pencils.

Split into two mixed-age teams. Give each team paper and pencils, and allow one minute – timed using the stopwatch – to write down 15 names from the Bible. The catch is that the names have to match the ones on the pre-prepared list!

Check the answers against the pre-prepared list that the leader has kept. Congratulate the winners!

Ask if anyone there has a name from the Bible, and talk about the stories that go with the name.

Connection: talk about the Bible as a collection of books, each of which contains stories of people. These stories are important – they help us to discover God and to know how to follow Jesus.

Explain the readings that happen in your local church on a Sunday: one from the Old Testament, which tells the story of how God's special people tried to follow his ways; one from the New Testament, which tells us about how the first Christians were working out how to live and behave as a church; and then one from the Gospels, which are the books that tell us all about Jesus' life and death.

Ask if anyone knows a story about Jesus they would like to share with everyone.

Explain that we can tell the story in lots of different ways, although all of them come from the Bible.

Tell an interactive Bible story (for example, from *The Lion Storyteller Bible* or the Naaman story from my book *Worship Together*[1] and so on).

Ask people what they liked or didn't like about the story/stories they have heard. Ask if they have any questions or if there is anything they are wondering about. Explain that usually someone stands up and gives a talk based on the questions and ideas that develop from the story – sometimes called the sermon. Ask if anyone would like to give a sermon!

Explain that we don't just have to find these stories when we are in church – it's a good idea to read them for ourselves at home as well.

Activity 4

— Weekly

Prayers for the world

Talk about prayer as part of the communion service, when we think about what we have heard and about the needs of the world. Explain that usually someone says words on our behalf, and we join in with a few words to show we are praying too:

Leader   Lord, in your mercy
All   **hear our prayer.**

Prayer activity

Invite each person to find a space by themselves.

Stretch up towards the roof, reaching hands as high as possible. Think about how amazing God is, and then pray that God's love will be known in all the world using these or similar words:

> Loving God, you love and care for all creation, for the world itself and the people who live here. We pray that in every place people will learn of that love. Be close to all those who work to share your love. Help them to be bold to speak out and caring to take actions.

Stretch arms out to the side and look at the windows. Think about all the people you know in the community outside and then pray for that community using these or similar words:

> Loving God, you know the needs of every person. We pray for this village/town and the people who live here, for our schools and our places of work; for our shops and the places we play. Be close to all those who are lonely or afraid, unwell or unhappy and help us to show others your love.

Lie down flat on the floor (or touch the walls). Think about the earth underneath you or the bricks in the walls; think about how long they have been here and how long God's people have gathered here. Pray for the people who gather in today's church in these or similar words:

> Loving God, we thank you for this special place and for all the people who help to take care of it every day. We pray that everyone who comes into this place will know that you are here and that all our worship and work will give glory to you.

Curl into a ball (or put head into hands). Invite everyone to be very still, so still they can hear or feel their own heart beating. In the stillness encourage people to pray for themselves that they will know that God is with them every moment of the day in every situation.

Invite everyone to jump up with a loud AMEN!

Ask the people to return to their seats. Recap briefly.

Activity 5

Memory game (we remember)

Invite everyone to sit in a large circle to play the memory game, which proceeds as follows:

- The first person says: 'Yesterday, I went to the shop and I bought [*something beginning with the letter "a", e.g. "apples"*].'

- The second person says: 'Yesterday, I went to the shop and I bought some apples and [*something beginning with the letter "b", e.g. "bagel"*].'

- The third person says: 'Yesterday, I went to the shop and I bought some apples, a bagel and [*something beginning with the letter "c", e.g. "cauliflower"*].'

Continue round the circle until the whole alphabet has been covered and someone can recite the whole shopping list of 26 items – one for each letter of the alphabet – in sequence.

Connection: talk about memory. One kind of remembering is remembering what to buy or what to take to school or jobs that need doing. But when we celebrate communion we are doing a different kind of remembering.

Activity 6

Memory box

You will need:

- a box that looks special – such as an old jewellery box or a shoe box covered in silver or gold paper – containing the following or similar items:

    - squeaky dog toy

    - significant stone or shell

    - a seaside postcard

    - a Christmas cracker

    - lots of loose chocolate buttons.

Without fully removing the lid of the box, squeak the dog toy. Ask people what it makes them think about – they will start telling puppy stories or tales about dogs they have owned. It's a different kind of remembering.

Repeat with other items – the stone or shell might be about a special place you have visited. The postcard should encourage thoughts about holidays; the cracker about Christmas memories.

Invite people to sniff inside the box. What does the smell remind them of? Then let them eat the chocolate as well.

Draw out the idea that there is a different kind of remembering – not just a list but the kind that takes us back to a time or a place. This is what Jesus meant when he said 'Remember me.' He didn't mean that we just had to remember his name but that we would remember everything he did and everything he means to us.

Talk about how the communion service is a celebration of all this. As we take communion we use all our senses and remember all that Jesus is for each of us.

Ending the session

Do a final recap of the circle that shows the shape of the communion service. Say something similar to:

> In this session we have been exploring what it means to gather as God's people, the church, where there is a place for everyone. We have thought about listening to God's word and praying for God's world.

> We have just begun to think about what it might mean to remember all that Jesus did for us, and how some things take us right back into events and what they mean to us.

Encourage people to think about things during the week ahead and come with any questions to the next session. Say something similar to:

> In the next session we will explore what it means to be ready to take communion; what happened when Jesus told us to take bread and wine and remember him; and we will think about what difference it might make to us in our lives.

Close with prayer.

Invite everyone to share refreshments.

Session 2 (2 hours)

Activity 1

For this opening activity you will need:

- an old sheet, or some lining paper or banqueting roll;
- lots of pictures about feasting and celebration (a practical tip: buy old recipe books in charity shops and use for food pictures or source them from the internet).

As people arrive, invite them to write, draw or stick pictures on to a large banner (which can be made from an old sheet or lining paper – practically, a sheet lasts longer but is harder to attach things to). You might like to use this as a 'celebration banner' later in the session, during Activity 4.

Gather everyone together.

Begin with:

Leader   The Lord be with you.
All   **And also with you.**

Talk about what was covered in the first session, and remind everyone that they all belong to God's people. This session will explore how we get ready ourselves, and why we do it, as well as what actually happens. Talk about the idea of remembering.

Activity 2

Doing wrong and making right

You will need:

- two (or more) A3 sheets of paper;

- pens.

Split the people into two – or more – mixed-age teams.

Give each team an A3 sheet of paper.

Invite them to:

- fold in half lengthways and press the fold firmly (at this point, people will wonder if they are doing origami!);

- unfold and notice that there are two columns;

- at the top of the left column draw a smiley face;

- at the top of the right column draw a sad face.

Give them one minute to write down in the right column as many things that people do wrong as they can think of – explain that it might be things they do themselves or things that happen in the world.

After one minute, swap to write down in the left column as many good things that people do that they can think of – again explain that it might be things they do or that happen in the world.

Get people to read out the good lists first. Talk about how fantastic it is when good things happen – like kind words, helpful actions and caring for others.

Read out the wrong things. Talk about how some of them are things we all do – maybe already this day some will have been cheeky, rude, lazy, selfish – and that's just the adults! Talk about how children are always having to say sorry – they fall out with friends and learn about making up; they disobey parents and have to put things right. It's not so easy for adults. Perhaps encourage one or two stories from across the age range.

Connection: when we come to communion we need to be right with God and with one another. It's a bit like washing your face and hands before going out to a party! We say sorry as we gather together, knowing that God always forgives us and lets us make a new start.

Activity 3

Forgiven

You will need:

- water in the font (or if not in church, use a large bowl of water)
- coloured paper squares (see Sheet 6.5, p. 56)
- pens for writing.

Invite everyone to gather around the font/bowl of water. Ask what it reminds them of – talk about baptism as the time when we set off on our journey as a follower of Jesus. The water reminds us that we can be forgiven and make a new start.

Invite everyone to make paper flowers, using the instructions on Sheet 6.5.

Place the flowers into the font and watch them open.

Invite everyone to look at their flower, and know that they are forgiven. If there is an authorized minister present, he or she might say the usual words of absolution used in your church, or use this form:

> May the Father forgive us
> by the death of his Son and strengthen us
> to live in the power of the Spirit
> all our days.
> **Amen.**[2]

Ask people to return to their seats. Remind them that the communion service is a celebration: we celebrate because we are forgiven, because of Jesus' love for us and because we are together. (If you wish you can mention other elements of the service here such as the Gloria, depending on your tradition and practice.)

Activity 4

Peace and parties

You will need:

- party poppers
- the large banner made you made for Activity 1 of this session (see page 46).

Introduce the words for sharing the peace and explain that sharing peace is about celebrating and remembering that we are one people, brought together because of God's love.

Let off party poppers and parade the celebration banner.

Ask everyone to share the peace with one another.

Activity 5

Giving back

You will need:

- an ordinary loaf of bread
- an ordinary bottle of wine
- either objects or pictures as follows:
  - shop counter (toy till/money)
  - lorry
  - factory
  - tractor
  - wheat/grapes
  - seeds/soil.

Hold up the bread and the bottle of wine: ask people where they came from and how you managed to get them – draw out idea of shops and money. Place objects or pictures on the floor.

Ask about how it got to the shop. Answer: lorry.

Ask where was it before that; talk about factories, bottling plants and so on.

Talk about farms and vineyards – tractor.

Talk about the crop in the field and finally the seeds.

Lay an object or picture down for each part of the discussion.

At the end, review the 'food chain' and talk about how everything is connected; how all kinds of people work together so that we have bread and wine on the table. (If your church takes a monetary offering at this point, talk about how that also represents our awareness that everything comes from God.)

Use the prayer normally used in your church when all the gifts have been gathered (offertory prayer), to give thanks for all that God does.

Activity 6

Setting the table

Note: This activity should take place in church.

Beforehand, you will need to:

- set up the table or altar as you would usually have it in your church for Holy Communion;
- make sure you have put all the items in place or nearby;
- lay out some vestments nearby (if you use them).

Invite everyone to gather around the table or altar.

Begin with a practical explanation of the various items on and around the table, getting adults and children to carry and name things. Each church may have variants on the tradition but this activity should include talking about 'setting the table' and using special items.

Encourage questions and discussion as different objects are brought out, making links to the idea of a special occasion at home when we sit at the table, make everything lovely and sit down together. Sometimes communion can be shared informally, just a few people in a circle, but explain what happens in your church on Sunday. Children enjoy discovering the right names for things; adults often see this as a kind of revision of things they learned years ago but have forgotten.

Things to talk about might include (depending on your tradition):

- corporal – a small cloth that makes a special area on the table; the bread and wine that are to be blessed are on this cloth

- purificators/lavabo towels/cruets and so on

- chalice – a special cup for holding wine: sometimes these are old and special to churches

- ciborium – a special covered chalice for holding the wafers/bread

- paten – a special plate for holding the bread/wafers

- colours of the church year; vestments that the ministers are wearing

- wafers/bread/wine.

Recap the ideas about remembering.

Explain that the priest/minister prays the special thank-you prayer, when we give thanks for Jesus and all he means to us.

Take time to tell the story of the Last Supper, emphasizing the four key actions:

On the night before he died, Jesus gathered with his friends. He took bread (*move a loaf to the centre*) and wine (*move a flagon – the container with the wine – to the centre*). Then he thanked God for the bread and the wine, and said that we should always remember him when we share bread and wine together. (*Lift hands in gesture of thanks/blessing.*) Then he broke the bread (*break the bread*) and poured the wine (*pour wine into a chalice*), reminding everyone of how he would give his life for everyone on the cross. Finally he gave the bread and the wine to everyone gathered round the table (*make a wide gesture to suggest sharing*).

Explain that the priest is praying aloud but usually there are parts that everyone joins in with – we are part of the prayer. At the end there might be some special words to say together, before everyone says 'Amen' very loudly.

Some churches' choirs sing the bits on behalf of all the people, so do whatever is most appropriate for the prayers used most often in your church. Practise!

Activity 7

Invitations

You will need enough envelopes containing invitations to hand out to everyone. Make them look special and important. The wording on the invitations should read 'Please come to the feast'.

Hand out the invitations.

Connection: talk about how we feel when we send and receive invitations.

Ask people to open their envelopes. Explain how we are invited to share in the feast that God is providing in bread and wine, and then we all say 'yes' to the invitation.

Explain that everyone is going to practise what happens when we take communion.

Use the words familiar in your church to invite everyone to come and share in the bread and wine.

Take some time to invite the children and their families to practise in the way normally used in your church. This might include kneeling at a rail, extending hands, trying (unconsecrated) wafers, receiving a chalice, tasting (unconsecrated) communion wine and learning when to return to your seat.

Take as much time as necessary at this point, to make sure everyone is comfortable and confident about what happens.

Activity 8

To go out into the world

You will need:

- a map of the world

- a map of your community

- a mirror – or anything safe that's more or less reflective – laid flat on the ground or table

- some small blank cards (flash cards or similar)

- pens.

Split the people into three groups and give them some of the blank cards.

Each group starts at one of the three objects.

At each place, write on the cards some of the needs for that area:

- at the world map – food in some countries, peace and an end to conflict;

- at the local map – their school, local hospital;

- at the mirror – for themselves.

Place the cards around the object.

After three minutes, each group moves to the right to the next object.

Repeat once more so that each group has visited every object.

Connection: God calls us to go out into the world and be like Jesus for other people. What kind of things can we do? What stops us and what encourages us?

Point out that taking communion, sharing in Jesus' life, gives us the strength to face the challenges in our own lives and to share God's light and love with others.

End with these words from the end of the baptism service:

Leader You have received the light of Christ;
          walk in this light all the days of your life.
All   **Shine as a light in the world
          to the glory of God the Father.**

Leader Go in the light and peace of Christ.
All   **Thanks be to God.**[3]

Conclusion

Recap briefly and summarize the key points. Then share food and friendship together.

Sheet 6.1: Getting-to-know-you chart (to use with Session 1, Activity 1 – see page 40)

Has lived in the same place all his/her life	Has a younger brother or sister	Has read all the Harry Potter books
Went to the same school as you	Sang or sings in a choir	Has seen the Queen in real life
Has never flown in an aeroplane	Plays a musical instrument	Has brown eyes
		Has a special teddy bear
Has visited three or more countries	Speaks a different language	Is the youngest in his/her family
	Has been a bell ringer	
	Has made a cake for a competition	
		Has hair shorter than yours

'Getting to know you' is all about speaking to lots of different people and finding out what you have in common.

The 'Getting-to-know-you' grid can be used in two ways:

Either give everyone a copy of the grid and invite them to get a different signature in each box. The first person to complete all the boxes wins.

Or give everyone a copy of the grid (or split the group into pairs) and invite them to get as many names as possible in each box. Set a time limit. When the time is up the winners are those with the most names overall.

Sheet 6.2: 'In the right order' (to use with Session 1, Activity 2 – see page 41)

heat oven	weigh ingredients	melt butter in saucepan
stir in oats	put in tray	cook in oven
cool and divide up	eat	

Sheet 6.3: 'The shape of the service A' (to use with Session 1, Activity 2 – see page 42)

Note: To increase the diameter of the circle to 28 cm, photocopy it on to A3 paper at 175 per cent.

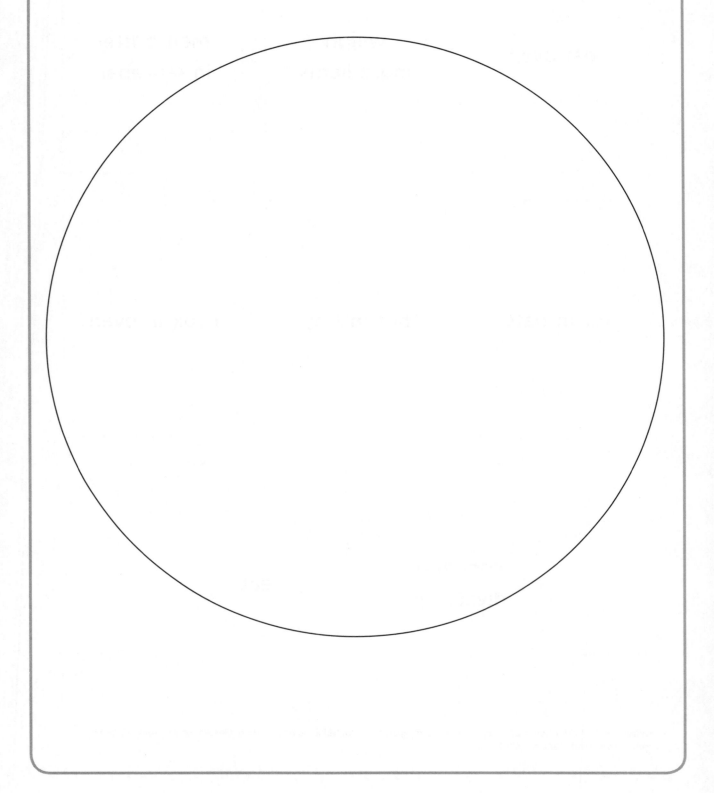

Sheet 6.4: 'The shape of the service B' (to use with Session 1, Activity 2 – see page 42)

Note: To increase the diameter of the circle to 28 cm, photocopy it on to A3 paper at 175 per cent.

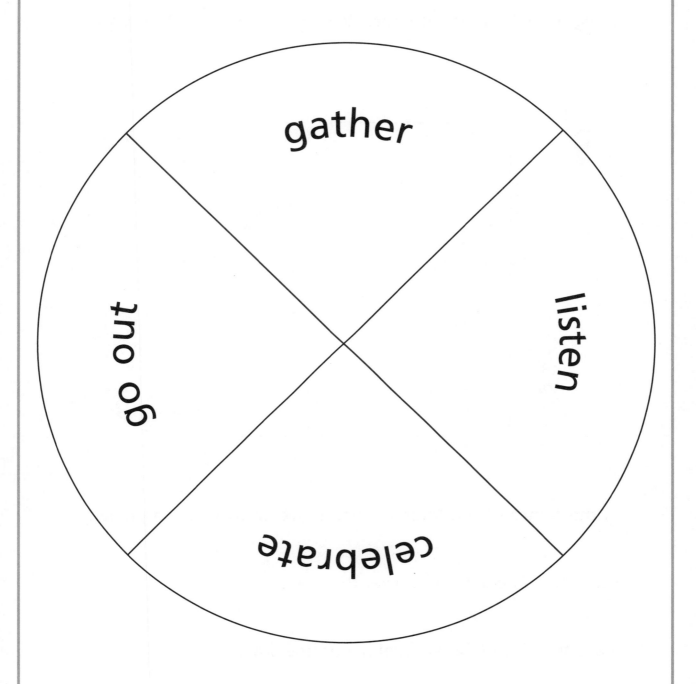

Sheet 6.5: Forgiven: water lily prayers (to use with Session 2, Activity 3 – see page 47)

Using a small square of paper, fold the corners into the centre.

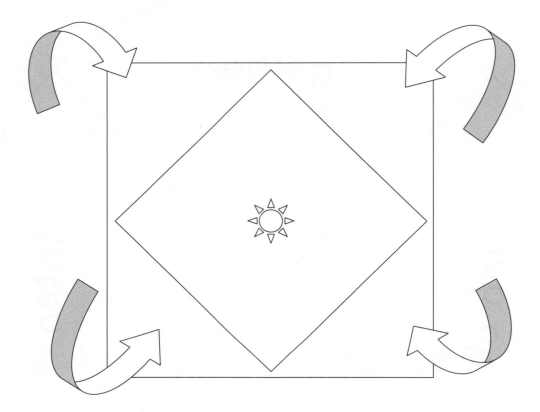

In the centre of the folded paper, write, draw or say a prayer.

Fold the corners in to conceal the prayer.

Place the folded paper carefully on the water.

Watch as the corners open like a flower to 'release' the prayer.

PART 4

Joining in

Including children in eucharistic worship

Sandra Millar

The family that eats together . . .

In recent years there has been a spate of scholarly and popular articles telling us that families who eat together stay together. Down the years there have been many memorable adverts that use this image to persuade us that just a little gravy, just a bit of ketchup will make family life smoother. By itself gravy does not create family life or bring love into being. But the reason advertisers use this scene is because deep down all of us know that time taken to sit with family across the generations is time well spent. Whether it was the 1980s gravy-loving family headed by Linda Bellingham or the contemporary family enjoying fish fingers, we are all captivated by the ideal of families eating together.

There are opinions from politicians and menus from chefs all suggesting that we should make more effort to sit down and spend time together. Many of us look back down the years to our own childhood and conjure memories of family tea times, Sunday roasts and holiday picnics. Still today, for many families, special occasions would not be complete without a family meal, even if the regular daily tea time has become fragmented by the busyness of diaries shot through with play dates, sports, clubs and coaching. Most of us cannot imagine Christmas Day without some kind of meal with the whole family gathered together, and there are other key times during the year, some particular to each family, some marking the passing of years. Getting family together really matters.

In the Jewish tradition, the Friday night Shabbat is still very much a family dinner, a time to include wider family, friends and newcomers together. It is a chance to pause and re-create, to step outside the mundane things of everyday life and rediscover thankfulness, companionship and the wider story of community. In her book *The Heavenly Party*,[1] Michele Guinness writes of the many ways eating and sharing together can be so much more than just food, but become transformed into occasions of healing and joy.

Jesus knew about how to bring people together around food, especially food in abundance. Two of the most well-known miracles are focused on a picnic lunch and a family wedding party, one the stuff of everyday life, the other one of life's party moments. In a field, Jesus ordered the disciples to sort out food for the gathering crowd of at least five thousand:

> 'Bring them here to me,' he said. And he told the people to sit down on the grass. Taking the five loaves and the two fish and looking up to heaven, he gave thanks and broke the loaves. Then he gave them to the disciples, and the disciples gave them to the people. They all ate and were satisfied, and the disciples picked up twelve basketfuls of broken pieces that were left over. The number of those who ate was about five thousand men, besides women and children.
>
> (Matthew 14.18–21, NIV)

In the account given in John's Gospel the presence of children is given added emphasis, as the basis of the meal for thousands is provided through the generosity of a small boy (John 6.8–9). There is nothing new about a family setting off for a day out with a bag packed ready for lunch. Some of my own best memories centre around picnics – planned and impromptu.

I was working in Kiev, not long after Ukraine opened up to Western churches. Life was still strange, and in a twist of logistics beyond most English conference organizers, after two days of a six-day event, we had to pack up and trek across the city to a new venue. When we arrived it was late in the evening and all the shops were closed. There was no food available in the school where we were to stay. The local organizers gathered us together in the hall and explained the situation to all 200 delegates. There was no food. However, he said, he knew that nearly everyone would have something with them – a soft drink, a packet of biscuits, a chocolate bar. So he invited us to meet in groups and pool all that we had and give thanks with joy.

My colleague and I – international guests for the weekend – went to our suitcases and dug out the emergency rations (at that time I was a seasoned international traveller and knew that a cereal bar could be a lifesaver!). We wandered into the group nearest our room and offered our English chocolate, savoury snacks and chewy mints. A family who had travelled by camper van shared cheese, bread and ham. Others brought tea and coffee and peanuts and dried fruits. It was a marvellous and memorable night, with laughter and joy and satisfied appetites: a family gathered around a meal.

Perhaps it is not surprising that the other memorable miracle took place at a wedding, the occasion that marks the transition from one family to another and the possibility of creating new customs and new relationships. The story of the Wedding at Cana, when Jesus transformed the everyday water into the wine of the kingdom, is alluded to at every Church of England wedding to this day. And the traditional name in our culture for a wedding reception is, of course, 'The Wedding Breakfast', and in other cultures is often known as the banquet or feast. It is a time for families to eat together in thanks and celebration.

But in fact it's not just eating together. As the chef and presenter Andy Bates put it, writing on the BBC website in February 2014, it's doing things together: 'the kind of families that eat together are also the kind that do other stuff together – and that is what makes them successful'.[2]

There is so much evidence that families who spend time together create strong and lasting bonds. A quick search on Google will reveal hundreds of websites with tips and ideas to encourage families to do things together, ranging from singing to storytelling, camping out, walking the dog or playing games. And the assumption in all these websites, family magazines and advice books is that family includes children. The idea behind both eating and doing things together is that the whole family benefits – toddlers and teenagers, parents and grandparents, and sometimes wider family members like aunties and godparents are included. Together is good is the clear message.

Which is why it seems so strange that the family of God find this so very difficult, for surely if human families flourish by spending time together in the everyday and the special times, then the family of the church will also benefit. Yet so many of our activities, social and worship, are split apart, divided across generations and age groups.

The picture of worship in the Old Testament is one of whole families gathering together, whether for times of discipline or times of celebration. For example, in Joel 2, one of the great Lenten readings, we find:

> Blow the trumpet on Mount Zion;
> give orders for a fast and call an assembly!
> Gather the people together;
> prepare them for a sacred meeting;
> bring the old people;
> gather the children
> and the babies too.
> Even newly married couples
> must leave their room and come.
> (Joel 2.15–16, GNB)

In Nehemiah, when the people gather to hear the book of Moses, the instruction is clear – the gathering is to include all who could understand what they heard, a group clearly different from the men and the women. But it is easy for us to overlook the fact that gatherings of 'all the people' would have included children. Somehow we have developed a kind of blinkered vision around words like 'everyone' and 'all' and 'people', unconsciously limiting the scope of these terms to adults only. Yet when God calls everyone, he means a huge, wide, all-embracing breadth, across race, culture, ability, gender and, yes, generations.

So it is a good thing for families to spend time together – a good thing too for the church family to worship, eat and play together, because it strengthens relationship, builds bonds of trust and creates community and reconciliation. It is the place where we can remember and retell the story of God's great saving love in Jesus Christ – and there is no place where we tell this with more power than in the Eucharist.

Including children in eucharistic worship: five key principles

But how can children be included in the Eucharist? Whenever I do training about all-age, fully inclusive, multi-generational worship, this question is raised as a special category. With a bit of thought we can begin to imagine a family service where there is the possibility of everyone worshipping together, but somehow the Eucharist seems a step too far. Yet the same principles that apply to good all-age communication and worship also apply to the Eucharist, which is always an occasion for the church family to be together and eat together.

There are **five key principles** that help worship to become effective for the whole people of God, and there may be one more that has particular importance when that worship becomes eucharistic.

1 Structure, pattern and repetition

Structure, pattern and repetition are key in enabling people to develop a sense of security and belonging. As we become familiar with what is expected, with the routines of work or social places, so we grow in confidence and the ability to engage. Almost everything we do as human beings has this sense of pattern and structure, whether it is the daily rituals of school or work place, or the behaviours needed to take part in a sports event or even a concert. We learn that when the bell rings at the theatre it's time to move to our seats; when the orchestra starts to tune up, we should fall quiet; when the lights go up again, the ice creams are on sale. We learn the rules of a team sport, both explicit and social. And each family will form its own rituals down the years, some to shape everyday life, some for special occasions like Christmas or Easter. In my family, we couldn't go downstairs on Christmas morning before Mum and Dad. In a friend's family, no presents are ever opened until after the Christmas Dinner, and for someone else Easter

breakfast would not be complete if there hadn't been a romp in the garden first, looking for eggs.

Repetition of behaviours and words helps us to absorb these into our subconscious, so that even years later, when minds and speech are failing, we find that we can still recall the words of the Lord's Prayer or raise trembling hands to receive bread and wine.

The Eucharist has a very strong structure, which has been explored in the short preparation course (see Chapter 6), and by using core texts frequently, families of all ages will build up a deep familiarity of words that will give strength and confidence in the years to come.

2 Making use of the senses and space

Making use of all our senses and of the space that we have is the second key principle, and again the Eucharist has within it all the potential for being multi-sensory and multi-spatial. It will almost always include a range of movement – standing and sitting, moving around for the peace, walking towards the altar and turning at different moments. However, these moments can be emphasized and other opportunities created. Readings can be creatively offered from different places, prayers can involve moving to stations, the shape of worship can be punctuated with processions and change in body position. The whole range of human senses can be used in prayers, whether prayers of penitence or prayers of intercession, as adults and children together engage with noise and silence, light and darkness, the perfume of candles or flowers, the touch of wood or stone and the taste of bread and wine. There is so much possibility for creativity in worship, and creativity engages people of all ages together.

3 Mystery and wonder

When I have been talking to congregations about admitting children to communion before confirmation, I often get the adults to write a list of words that come to mind when they think about communion. When we share these lists together, there are certain words that occur frequently across all sorts of places and congregations. Often these are words about belonging and community, but even more frequently they are words about mystery and wonder, about awe and a sense of amazement at the gift that is offered. And mystery and wonder are another of the key elements of good all-age communication.

Throughout this book we have been thinking about how the gift of Christ in bread and wine is an awe-inspiring mystery of God's grace. Receiving communion is not dependent on our intellectual understanding or our good behaviour but is simply about accepting the invitation that is extended to us to share in the life of Christ. So mystery and wonder is at the heart of the Eucharist, and children of all ages are frequently touched by that mystery.

In one very large church, where the Eucharist is celebrated with a lot of symbol and ceremony, younger children and their adults were invited to come close around the table as the great Eucharistic Prayer was offered. They were sitting on hassocks and bean bags, clustered close, and even very little ones watched with intensity as the minister reverently moved his hands, raised the chalice and broke bread. The mystery was being enacted in front of them and, beyond words, they were sensing it and participating in it.

I was discussing communion with an eight-year-old boy and what it meant to him. He said: 'It is the presence of Jesus, God's gift for all of us.' In fact that sentence doesn't carry the full weight of meaning for him written down – say the word 'presence' out loud; then say the word 'presents' out loud. When your are eight or nine, 'presence' isn't part of your everyday language but 'presents' surely is! And he had interpreted rightly, blending the two words together as he thought about the mystery of bread and wine, which is truly God's gift for everybody.

4 Universal themes and stories

There are certain stories that reach out across generations and touch the minds and hearts of young and old alike. As a grown woman I can read *Guess How Much I Love You*[3] – a tale designed to be read by parents to little ones – and find myself moved to tears by that last whisper, 'I love you right up to the moon – AND BACK.' Why? Because the story of abundant love is relevant to people of every age. We all need to know that someone loves

us more than we can ever imagine. Good all-age communication has at its core **universal themes and stories** that matter at every stage of life. We grapple with questions of failure and love and acceptance and disappointment whether we are 4 or 44 or 84. The story that lies at the core of every eucharistic celebration is a universal story – it is the remembering and re-enacting of human failure and of God's huge love reaching to us, love that is willing to lay down life so that we can be safe and saved. The simple, profound truth of this story is relevant to every stage, so celebrating the Eucharist is intrinsically inclusive of all ages.

5 Leadership

However, beyond all these key elements, there is something else that needs to happen. The Eucharist is celebrated by the whole people of God, but we are led through the celebration by the minister, usually called the president in the Church of England. It is the president who will enable the worship to be fully inclusive, and it is when he or she intentionally sets out to include everyone that worship becomes a true family occasion. Some people seem to do this instinctively and effortlessly, but for most it requires a conscious decision to call to mind that this worship is for everyone present – including the babies, the boisterous children, the unsmiling teenagers and the demure adults. **Leading** all-age worship is a skill, and throughout the service there will be moments when there are words and actions intentionally aimed at including those of different generations, whether younger or older, and those of different abilities – pre- and post-readers, physically active or not, talkers and reflectors, children and adults.

Involving children: roles and responsibilities

But there is a particular way celebrating the Eucharist can be fully inclusive for children.

For children, especially those aged between 5 and 11, having real responsibility and an opportunity to take part is a real way of making them involved and engaged. There are many points in the Eucharist where children can take part, alongside their inclusion in receiving bread and wine. In fact everything that might be done by a lay adult can be done by a child (with the exception of distribution – at the time of writing, only those aged 16 and older can be chalice assistants, although this is under consideration by the General Synod).

Here are some suggestions about how children and young people might be involved in the celebration of the Eucharist.

Before the service

Children can be involved as sidespeople, welcomers and assistant vergers, helping to put out the things needed for the service. Children can also be involved as musicians and singers, and in many churches will be part of the choir or perhaps an orchestra.

The gathering

If there is a procession to begin the service, children may have particular roles, especially in those traditions where there are usually servers. Children can be acolytes (candle-bearers) or even crucifers (carrying the cross). One church I know keeps a special short, light, wooden cross and encourages children from the age of about four upwards to learn to carry this and lead a procession. Watching a seven-year-old and her special friend working together to carry this cross with concentration and solemnity serves as a reminder of the breadth of God's call to serve – we are all his disciples. Even where formal serving is not part of the tradition, inviting children and their adults to be part of a procession to start a service is a good way of including and welcoming everyone. This might be for a special festival or it might be a routine part of Sunday worship.

If there is any special praise or opening prayer that is responsive, children may introduce these words or lead the congregation in the responses.

Saying sorry

Children and young people may say the sentences that introduce a Kyrie (Lord, have mercy) confession and take part in leading or helping with any creative response. In one church, each person was given a small stone to hold during the confession, and then some of the children went and gathered them in and brought them to the table as a sign of letting go of things for which we are sorry.

Listening together

Children and young people can read and help interpret the readings alongside the adults. This may involve rehearsal and building confidence, but there are many excellent readers around eight to ten years old in our congregations, and at this age children have not yet developed the self-consciousness that can make it embarrassing for teenagers to be asked to read in public. I was about to step forward in a small rural church to read the Gospel when the churchwarden approached and, in a stage whisper, asked if I would mind a child reading. Of course, I said, but was somewhat alarmed when a small girl of about seven stepped forward clutching a tiny zipped Bible, clearly a King James version. I should not have worried. Her reading of the story of Peter walking on the water still lives in my mind as one of the best readings I have ever heard!

Responding

Children may lead the people in the prayers of intercession, which can be a great opportunity to use imagination, movement and a multi-sensory approach. It is important that children are given the opportunity to lead, not simply to perform prayers they have written. Adults have a great tendency when children read prayers to stop praying themselves and watch, applauding – internally or externally – the children for their cleverness, cuteness or behaviour. This is not the same as leading the prayers. Intercession is the space when the whole people of God join in praying for the Church, the world and the community, and in this children are very capable.

The peace

Children may be invited to share in offering the words of invitation to the peace, either by standing alongside the president or by joining in with the words. For many children and young people, taking part in the peace is a significant part of the Eucharist, giving them an opportunity to move, to share and to feel included, as well as a real chance to minister to others across generations.

The offertory

Children may bring up the gifts and help to set the table, doing everything a server does. This can be a very special opportunity for families to do something together as well, and is a task children take on with great seriousness. At a major festival Eucharist in a cathedral, where the Archbishop of Canterbury was presiding, children were included as much as possible. A group of youngsters, aged from 7 to 14, helped set the table, carrying chalices and patens with great care and precision. Many commented on how moving they found this routine and simple action. It is also possible for children to lead the offertory prayer, in particular the prayer 'With this bread that we bring'. Sometimes it may be that a family should say this together.

If children are involved in setting the table, careful thought needs to be given to when and where they go after helping. It can look very strange to invite them to help and then send them away again, and it is possible to keep them standing close around the table.

The Eucharistic Prayer

While the prayer is clearly said by the president, some of the prayers do give opportunities for children to be involved. Prayer D in *Common Worship* has a clear refrain running through it, which can be said by children before the congregation join in with the response:

Children This is our story,
All   **this is our song.**

The additional Eucharistic Prayers for use when the majority present are children were approved for use in 2013.[4] Many churches find these prayers helpful to use on occasions where lots of families will be present for the Eucharist, as well as for school Eucharists. Both prayers have clear opportunities for children to join in, to ask questions and to take part in responses.

The invitation, distribution and so on

If children have been involved in preparing the table and serving at the altar, they should be treated just as other servers are treated, receiving communion as part of an altar party or according to the tradition of the church. It might also be appropriate to include children standing alongside the adults who are distributing communion, especially where communion is distributed from

'standing stations'. Children and young people might also be involved in other activities at this point, for example, placing prayers on a prayer tree or being part of music being offered.

After communion

Children may be part of saying any dismissal words or distributing items in the congregation. This often happens at times like Mothering Sunday, when flowers are given away, but could happen on other occasions too, when the congregation are being asked to take something with them as they leave.

Recessional

Include children in any movement at the end and involve them in helping with the hospitality and activities needed at the end of the worship service.

Participation is a key to helping children feel part of the family and discovering what it means to be a worshipper and a minister, in the sense that everyone is called to share in worship and ministry. In school and home children take on their share of the work that needs to be done, whether that is in simple helping or in bigger discussions like helping with interviewing new staff. At one level, movement and activity enable children to engage, but at another this is modelling for all of us the inclusive nature of God's invitation to all of us to remember through bread and wine.

Do children have to be present at every Eucharist?

Once children are receiving communion, it will be as important for them to receive as it is for adults.

However, all of us need peer-group learning and peer-group time as well as family time. While it is clearly good for relationships and community for people to spend time across generations, we also know that it is good for us to be challenged and encouraged in ways appropriate to our age group.

Not every meal in a household will be for everyone all the time – sometimes there are children's parties and after-school tea and sometimes there are adult 'date nights' with candlelit dinners. The important thing is that at the heart of the family is time spent together.

Children and adults in the church family also need peer-group time, when they can think about being disciples in ways appropriate to them. It may well be good for children to have their own time during the sermon, when the adults are being given teaching suited to them. It may also be that sometimes children go to their own sessions earlier and explore things like saying sorry or intercessory prayer in ways that reflect what is happening in their lives.

It is probably good practice for children to be with the whole family at least on major celebrations, and then work out a pattern that seems good in the local context. However, ideally children should return from peer-group learning at the peace, sharing that moment with the whole church family.

An outline service for admitting children to Holy Communion

Sandra Millar

Introduction

Before we can engage with the question of children receiving communion regularly (as discussed in the previous chapter), there will come a time when, after a preparation course, children will receive for the first time. And one of the issues that often emerges during discussions with PCCs about admitting children to communion before confirmation is the whole question of 'first communion'. Many of us have shadowy memories, either from experience, through friends or fiction, of an emotionally loaded occasion, involving special frocks and special presents.

> The great day came at last . . . Everything she put on that morning was new and white. A white prayer-book and a mother-of-pearl rosary, a gift from Reverend Mother, lay beside her new veil, and the stiff wreath of white cotton roses that every First Communicant wore. They walked into the chapel two by two, pacing slowly up the aisle like twelve brides, to the sound of swift, lacy music.[1]

These shadowy memories and half-formed ideas are largely drawn from a very traditional Roman Catholic experience, but somehow linger on in our minds. This might be one of the questions that has come up during your preliminary discussions, but contemporary Church of England customs are very different, and neither congregation nor families need worry about expense or presentation.

The children who are to be admitted will usually first receive communion in the course of an ordinary Sunday Eucharist. Sometimes it may be right to choose a significant festival, especially if there is a small group of children being admitted at the same

time. Families are encouraged to invite godparents and grandparents along, and all the congregation is encouraged to pray and support the children as they continue their journey of faith and discipleship.

The Church of England has provided some liturgical resources that can be used on such an occasion, and these can be found in *Common Worship: Christian Initiation*.[2] The *Common Worship* liturgy offers some suggestion for words of introduction, a welcome and sentences for the peace and the intercessions. There are also some questions that can be asked of those being admitted, but these are optional.

During the service it may well be appropriate for those children to be specially recognized in some way and to receive a certificate and perhaps a gift, such as a Bible or prayer book. An ideal time to do this might be just before the peace, so that the children can be part of sharing the peace. At the distribution of communion the children could come up with their families, perhaps receiving first, but equally they could simply receive in the normal flow of the congregation.

It is important that a register be kept of those who are admitted to communion before confirmation, and the certificate may be important if families move to other areas where they are not familiar with children as communicants. However, once a child has been admitted, he or she cannot be turned away at a church that doesn't admit children to communion before confirmation.

As with every time God's people gather to celebrate the Eucharist, this service should be for everyone and will follow the same pattern as all other communion services.

- The people will gather together and prepare themselves for worship by saying sorry to God and praising him for his forgiveness.

- Everyone listens to and explores God's word, either together or with a peer group.

- Everyone responds to that word – by declaring faith and praying for God's world.

- Everyone celebrates as bread and wine are brought forward and Jesus' offering for us

all is remembered in the great Eucharistic Prayer.

- After receiving communion, everyone is sent out to share the good news in the world.

The following is an outline for a liturgy that could be used when children are being admitted to communion, but could also be used on other occasions to help the whole congregation explore together the meaning of the Eucharist.

An outline liturgy for admission to Holy Communion: remembering Jesus

When a church has been exploring what it means to admit children to communion before confirmation, it may be helpful, either before or after the discussions, to have a Sunday Eucharist for all ages where the meaning and purpose of communion is explored by the whole church family. It provides a great opportunity for children to take part and share some of their insights and gifts with the wider congregation. Alternatively, some of these resources might be used at a service where children are to receive communion for the first time. The alternative Gospel reading might be used, or the lectionary readings for the day might be used, as the talk will pick up on themes from the eucharistic liturgy rather than the readings.

Key lectionary readings

Note: The authorized lectionary readings have to be used at key festivals and seasons in the Church of England.[3]

Luke 22.7–20 (21–27), 'The special meal'

 ## WE GATHER

Opening hymn

Informal welcome

During the welcome, the minister or a child explains that this service is to help us think about communion.

Voice   Come, everyone who thirsts, come to the waters;
come, everyone without money, come eat;

come buy wine and milk, without money, without price!
For God would feed you with the finest of the wheat,
with honey from the rock, he will fill you up.

(*All stand.*)

Everyone is welcome to the feast. Will you come?

All   **We will come!**

Voice   Everyone has a place at the table. Will you come?

All   **We will come!**

Voice   Everyone belongs to God's family. Will you come?

All   **We will come!**

Voice   Everyone here is welcome. Everyone here is invited. Everyone here belongs to God's people.

(*Invite everyone to join hands, then to raise them high.*)

All   **Amen. Amen. Amen.**

We say sorry

Making connections

Minister   Whenever we come together to worship in God's presence, we take some time to put right things in our own lives. These might be things we have done to hurt other people, or things we have forgotten to do as we try to follow the way of Jesus.

If you have children who have recently been prepared to receive communion, invite them to explain how saying sorry to God is a way of getting ready to share together.

Invite everyone to stand and curl hands into a ball.

Voice Forgive us for holding things too tightly and forgetting to share.
Lord have mercy

All **Lord have mercy.**

Invite everyone to cross their arms.

Voice Forgive us for not showing friendship and help to other people.

Christ have mercy

All **Christ have mercy.**

Invite everyone to turn towards the back of church.

Voice Forgive us for all the times we turn away from you and ignore your voice.
Lord have mercy

All **Lord have mercy.**

Invite everyone to turn towards the font.

Minister Hear the word of grace in Jesus Christ:
The love of God for us never fails.
Nothing can separate us from that love.
Rise up, know you are forgiven, and live in freedom and faith. Amen.

Hymn/Gloria

Collect or prayer for the day

Voice Loving God,
who, through the gifts of bread and wine,
invites us all to remember
the death of your Son, Jesus Christ,
help us to share in his life
and show his love to all around us
as we follow you day by day;
through Jesus Christ our risen Lord,

All **Amen.**

 # WE LISTEN

Minister or child Please sit. Now we are ready to hear the story of God's work in the world. Today we are hearing about how Jesus first told us we would remember him always through bread and wine.

Reading(s)

The key reading is the reading from Luke, which should be read in the usual way before the talk, and which retells the story and invites the congregation to reflect.

Talk

Spread out a large table-cloth-sized piece of yellow fabric. Talk about what yellow makes us think of and how the colour makes us feel. Draw out the idea that yellow is a colour of celebration and friendship. For this day it is going to represent a time when Jesus gathered with all his friends for a special meal, a meal that was a celebration every year.

Then take a large dark-coloured piece of fabric – such as navy – and slowly roll it into a ball.

Ask how the dark colour makes people think and feel. Draw out the idea that dark colours make us think of dark times. Jesus was gathered with his friends for a celebration called Passover. It was about remembering sad times and happy times – invite people to talk to one another about similar times in their lives. Say something similar to:

Jesus and his friends were remembering how God set his people free from slavery.

But then Jesus changed everything.

Talk about how Jesus took bread and thanked God and then took wine and thanked God:

He blessed the bread and the wine.

Spread out a large table-cloth-sized piece of red fabric. Pause and ask everyone to be quiet as they think about what the colour red makes us think of, and then invite people to talk to one another.

Draw out the idea of blood and anger and love:

Jesus took bread and wine, thanked God, blessed the bread and wine, broke the bread, and invited everyone to share with him.

He told all his friends that eating bread and drinking wine would be a special way of remembering him. This is not just remembering something for school or the shopping list, but the kind of deep remembering that takes us back to a situation.

Invite people to share with one another what taking communion means to them.

End by reminding them that everyone is included in the invitation to share in Jesus' death on the cross, the way to new life.

WE RESPOND

Creed or statement of faith

Making connections

Minister We've thought about how we are all God's family and we are all invited to share in the life and death of Jesus as we take bread and wine. Let's remind ourselves of the things we believe as we say:

All **We believe in God the Father, from whom every family in heaven and earth is named.**

We believe in God the Son, who lives in our hearts through faith, and fills us with his love.

We believe in God the Holy Spirit, who strengthens us with power from on high.[4]

Prayers

Voice As part of our response to God's word, we turn and pray for God's world.

Invite people to visit four stations in the church to offer their prayers. Play music while this happens, such as the Taizé chant, 'Eat this bread, drink this cup', by Jacques Berthier, or something similar.

Station 1

On a small table, place a range of things to represent some of the gifts in the life of your church, including bread and wine, music, thinking, speaking, sports, baking and so on.

Place a card with the word 'take' and, on several cards for people to pick up, print out the first verse of the hymn 'Take my life and let it be' (which can be found in a variety of hymn books, including *Common Praise*, *Mission Praise* or *The English Hymnal*). Place a bowl of water on or near the table (or if space permits, place near the font).

Print out these instructions:

There are many gifts in the world, in the church and in our own lives. Take a moment to pray that God will take all the gifts in this place and use them, praying especially that God will use your life. Then make a sign of the cross on your hands using the water.

Station 2

On a table, place some pictures of the community where you live, families, friends, school, work and so on. Place a small bowl with confetti on or near the table.

Place a card with the word 'bless' on the table.

Print out these instructions:

Take a handful of confetti and scatter it around the photographs. Thank God for those you live with, learn with, work with and play with, and ask God to bless those places and people.

Station 3

On a table, place some newspapers and other media with stories of those who are struggling. Include a list of those in your community who are being prayed for. On the table also place a bowl containing paper hearts large enough to write or draw on, along with pens. Also have a large map of the world nearby, and a card with the word 'broken'.

Print out these instructions:

There are many people and places in our world that are broken and in need – hungry, homeless, hurting. Take a moment to write or draw your prayer on a heart and then place it on the world map as you pray for God's love to heal the broken.

Station 4

On a table, place some bowls of things to share – sweets and fruits, even a pile of pennies, a Bible or other resources. Make some paper hands – you could just draw round your own hand, flat and open. Place the hands next to a large sheet of paper, such as A1 flip-chart paper (if space permits, you could attach the sheet to a door or window). Provide some means of sticking the hands to the paper.

Print out these instructions:

God asks us to go into the world and share the good news of his love with other people. First take something from one of the bowls and share it with someone nearby, thinking about how it feels when someone is kind and generous to us. Then pick up a paper hand and stick it on the large sheet of paper, praying as you do so that this church will be a place of sharing and welcome.

After everyone has visited the stations and returned to their seats, a young person or other minister gathers all the prayers together:

Voice   Lord God, we try to hear your voice and to hear the needs of your world. You promise to hear our prayers as we gather together. Hear our prayers today.

All   Amen.

OR

An alternative prayer activity

If your church is not able to set up stations, then use the idea here.

* Ask some people beforehand to be ready with small baskets or bowls in which they will collect up the tags at the end of the activity.

* If people are not seated in pews or rows, make sure they are in small groups.

* Hand round to each person a small gift tag or similar item.

* Invite everyone to hold the gift tags during the prayers and follow the actions.

* Ask them to place the gift tags on one hand, and cover them with the other.

* Invite the people to think about the gifts that are in the church and in their own lives, and to pray using the following or similar words.

Minister Loving God, we thank you for all the riches you have given us – the special gifts that each person has here in this place. For people who can sing, help, care, speak; for those who help us when we cry and those who make us laugh for joy. Take all the gifts we have here and use them, we pray. Lord, hear our prayer,

All   Please.

Ask the people to open their hands, and open up the gift tags. Encourage them to think about all the places in the community where they go during the week. Pray using these or similar words:

Minister Loving God, we pray for all the places around us – for our schools, our work, our shops, our homes, and we ask that you bless them with the light of your love. We thank you for everyone who helps and encourages us. Help and encourage them, we pray.
Lord, hear our prayer

All **Please.**

Invite the people to tear the gift tags in halves or quarters. Encourage them to think about all the places in the world where there are people struggling with war, poverty, pain or injustice. Pray using these or similar words:

Minister Loving God, we pray that you come close with your love to all who are hurting today, to those in nations where there is violence or hunger, and to those we know in our own lives who are sad or in pain. Draw close to each person in every place and give them your peace, we pray.
Lord, hear our prayer,

All **Please.**

Ask everyone to swap their torn gift tags with someone nearby. Think about your church and how it can share the good news of Jesus' love in different ways, whether locally or through the diocese.

Minister Loving God, we pray that you strengthen us in your church, and give us courage to go out into the world and share the good news of your love with other people. Help us to be a place of welcome and to be people who care for others, we pray.
Lord, hear our prayer,

All **Please.**

Finally, invite people to pass the torn gift tags to whoever has the small baskets or bowls (see the bullet list just above). Once all have been collected, bring them to the front.

Voice Lord, hear all our prayers today, we pray.

All **Amen.**

Admission of children to communion

Invite those who are being admitted to come forward.

Minister We are God's people, gathered in this place, called to share in his love, and know his presence in bread and wine.

Will you, parents, godparents and all the church family, continue to worship and learn together, supporting *N* together as we grow in faith and love?

All **We will.**

Invite everyone to pray.

Minister Loving God, we pray for *N* and ask that they may know you are with them every day, and that your presence is with them in every situation. Help them to be confident to share in your life and courageous in sharing that life with others. Amen.

You might want to give a gift or certificate at this point.[5]

The peace

The minister, together with the children, introduces the peace, using these or similar words:

Minister and children **God makes peace within us – let us claim it. God makes peace between us – let us share it.**

Minister The peace of the Lord be with you

All **and also with you.[6]**

Preparing the table

If possible, you could involve the children at this point (see pages 61–4 for further information about involving children).

Prayer: offering the gifts

This prayer may be said by children/families.

Minister With this bread that we bring

All **we shall remember Jesus.**

Minister With this wine that we bring

All **we shall remember Jesus.**

Minister Bread for his body,
wine for his blood, gifts from God to his table we bring.

All **We shall remember Jesus.**[7]

The Eucharistic Prayer

It might be appropriate to use one of the Additional Eucharistic Prayers for use with children present, or alternatively Prayer D ('This is his story'), which is very responsive.[8]

The Lord's Prayer

Breaking of bread

(It is not necessary to include an Agnus Dei.)

Invitation

Distribution of communion

Post-communion prayer

Minister Lord,
we have broken your bread
and received your life.

By the power of your Spirit
keep us always in your love;
through Jesus Christ our Lord.[9]

 # WE GO OUT

Notices may be included at this point as part of moving the focus to our Christian lives.

'We go into the world' may be said by the minister or others.

Invite everyone to turn and face the door, which should be flung open. Someone could ring a bell (like a town crier).

Voices Listen everyone, there's a place for everyone with God's people.
As we go out, we pray that people will come in.
As we come in we pray that we will bring others with us.
As we go out and as we come in, Jesus is with us!
Go in peace to love and serve the Lord.
Thanks be to God!

Blessing

Minister May the peace of Jesus be in your hearts.
May the joy of Jesus be on your lips.
May the hope of Jesus be in your life.
And the blessing of God . . .

All **Amen.**

The dismissal

Minister Go in peace to love and serve the Lord.

All **Thanks be to God.**

Additional prayers, liturgy and ideas for all-age eucharistic worship

Nick Harding

The Eucharist, whether it takes place in a school or church, should be as inclusive as possible. This means it should have language that children and adults can understand, and be accessible for those who do not regularly attend.

The Church of England has devised two Eucharistic Prayers that involve a little more participation and repetition than the communion prayers most worshippers are familiar with. They are for use where a significant number of children and young people are present for the service, and there is an additional booklet called *Common Worship: Additional Eucharistic Prayers*.[1] This contains notes on authorization, as well as additional guidance on how to use the new prayers creatively. One of the key points to note is that it is entirely in order for children to prepare and write prayers, and in particular some 'proper prefaces', to freshen up the set liturgy.

This selection of ideas and prayers could be used to enhance the prescribed and authorized liturgy, with the aim of breathing new life and interaction into what should always be an important and reverent occasion. The sections are as follows:

1 Coming to worship together

2 Seeking God's forgiveness

3 Listening to God's story

4 Remembering the special meal

5 Thanking God for his goodness

1 Coming to worship together

Leader All over the world Christians gather to share something special together.

All **They remember.**

Leader They remember God's love for them.

All **They remember.**

Leader They remember how Jesus lived and died and rose again.

All **They remember.**

Leader They remember that he told them to do something special.

All **They remember.**

Leader They remember to share bread and wine together.

Leader Here at . . . . we are gathered to share something special together.

All **We remember.**

Leader We remember God's love for us.

All **We remember.**

Leader We remember how Jesus lived and died and rose again.

All **We remember.**

Leader We remember that he told them to do something special.

All **We remember.**

Leader We remember, and so we share bread and wine together.

Belonging

Ask everyone to talk to the person next to them about what they belong to and/or support. Encourage the adults to include and listen to children. Suggestions may include sports teams, schools, church groups, Mothers' Union and so on. Then ask whether anyone has anything to show what they belong to – membership cards, t-shirts, uniforms. In each of those groups there are lots of different people who have something in common. Everyone is different, but everyone belongs. So it is with us gathered here – we all belong, whatever our age, interests or needs.

Reflection

Ask everyone to put their hands out in front of them with their palms up. This is a sign of both receiving and giving. Then say these sentences, allowing a little time for silent reflection after each:

> We hold our hands open to receive our invitation to the special meal. How do we feel?
>
> We are part of God's chosen people, whom he wants to bless. How do we feel?
>
> We are able to offer ourselves to God in return. Are we willing to?

Leader We are all together,

All **we are all together,**

Leader and we are all different,

All **we are all together,**

Leader and we have many good things,

All **we are all together,**

Leader and we are of many ages and backgrounds,

All **we are all together,**

Leader and we have many needs,

All **we are all together,**

Leader and we are very different,

All **we are all together,**

Leader and we are all united,

All **we are all together,**

Leader and we worship God together,

All **we are all together,**

Leader and we thank you, God.

2 Seeking God's forgiveness

There are many authorized confessions and absolutions in *Common Worship*, and they can be used alongside these prayers and activities.

Making it right

Ask the congregation if they have ever broken something special. Ask for a few suggestions from them. Then ask about other things that might be broken, like friendships. How does it feel when we break our friendships by hurting our friend? Sometimes we are the ones who do the breaking; sometimes other people hurt us and make us unhappy.

When we go wrong and do bad things, we break our relationship with God, but he is always ready to forgive those who really turn to him, and want to make it right.

It is true!

Leader You forgive all people who turn to you:

All **it is true!**

Leader You are here with us now:

All **it is true!**

Leader You take all the things we have done wrong:

All **it is true!**

Leader You take all of our guilt:

All **it is true!**

Leader You make us new and fresh:

All **it is true!**

Leader You forgive all people who turn to you:

All **it is true!**

Giving it to God

You will need two bin bags – and two people to carry them around – and lots of small pieces of paper. One piece of paper should be given to every member of the congregation.

God offers us the chance to give him the things we feel guilty about or sorry for. Look at your piece of paper, and imagine you have drawn or written on it the thing or things that you know you've done that you shouldn't have over the past few days. Now screw the paper up, and as one of the bin bags comes near you, throw the screwed-up paper into it.

Because you forgive . . .

Leader Let's sit and think about the things we have said that we shouldn't have.
(*pause*)
Because you forgive,

All **we are forgiven.**

Leader Let's spend a moment remembering things we have done that were wrong.
(*pause*)
Because you forgive,

All **we are forgiven.**

Leader So we think now of things we have not done that we should have.
(*pause*)
Because you forgive,

All **we are forgiven.**

Leader And now we remember people who have been hurt by us.
(*pause*)
Because you forgive,

All **we are forgiven.**

Leader Each time we go wrong we hurt God, our maker.
(*pause*)
Because you forgive,

All **we are forgiven.**

We forgive as you forgive

Say this prayer line by line, with the congregation repeating each line. If possible keep the rhythm going, to add life to the words. Children and young people could be invited and encouraged to learn and deliver the 'leader' line.

Leader Thank you that you welcome us back.

All **Thank you that you welcome us back.**

Leader Thank you that you always forgive.

All **Thank you that you always forgive.**

Leader We can all have a fresh new start.

All **We can all have a fresh new start.**

Leader Help us to remember your love.

All **Help us to remember your love.**

Leader Help us all to forgive like you.

All **Help us all to forgive like you.**

Leader We forgive as you forgive.

All **We forgive as you forgive.**

3 Listening to God's story

Christians of all ages grow in knowing more about God's love through reading and listening to the Bible. The stories and songs in the Bible make a difference to people. Two stand-alone activities are suggested; they can also be done one after another.

Prayer before the Bible reading

Leader Help us, God, to hear your story.

All **Help us listen to your word.**

Leader Help us, God, to understand your story.

All **Help us listen to your word.**

Leader Help us, God, to remember your story.

All **Help us listen to your word.**

And again

Read the Bible story out loud twice. The first time it should be as written, but the second time add a few mistakes. Explain this to the congregation before the first time through, and ask them to raise their hands or shout out 'Stop!' when they hear a mistake.

What I see

Give each person a sheet of paper and a pencil. Read the Bible story twice, asking everyone to listen with their eyes closed the first time through. Then, for the second time, ask them to open their eyes and draw or write on the paper anything that the story makes them think of, a word or scene that stood out for them, and so on.

These words or pictures could be shared and discussed for a short time in small groups if that seems to suit the context.

Prayer after the Bible reading

For the prayer after the Bible reading, devise simple actions for the phrase 'your story'. Pointing up for 'your' and forming hands to look like an open book for 'story' would suffice. Ask everyone to do the actions each time you say 'your story'.

> Dear God, thank you for *your story*.
>
> Thank you for the messages in *your story*.
>
> Thank you that we can learn from *your story*.
>
> Thank you for the love you give in *your story*.
>
> Thank you that sharing bread and wine is part of *your story*.
>
> Thank you that there's no end to *your story*.
>
> Thank you that I am part of *your story*.

4 Remembering the special meal

Proper prefaces

This liturgical prayer comes before the Eucharistic Prayer, and takes the form of prayers of thanks for what God has done and what Jesus means to us. Either before the service individually or in groups, members of the congregation could devise and prepare their own prayers. To help, they could begin with the phrase 'And so we give you thanks . . .'.

Special meals

Ask the people to sit quietly with their eyes closed. Perhaps have some quiet music playing while you do this reflection.

Think about when you get together for a special meal:

- What do you eat at the special meal?
- What happens around the table?
- What do you remember about it after the meal?
- What is special about the communion meal?
- What does it make you think of?
- What do you remember after the meal?

The bread and wine

Leader Later, this bread will be shared.

All **Thank you for the bread, living Lord.**

Leader Later, we will remember Jesus giving his body.

All **Thank you for the bread, living Lord.**

Leader Later, we will share in Jesus' pain.

All **Thank you for the bread, living Lord.**

Leader Later, we will share in Jesus' rising to new life.

All **Thank you for the bread, living Lord.**

Leader Later, this wine will be shared.

All **Thank you for the wine, living Lord.**

Leader Later, we will remember Jesus giving his blood.

All **Thank you for the wine, living Lord.**

Leader Later, we will share in Jesus' pain.

All **Thank you for the wine, living Lord.**

Leader Later, we will share in Jesus' rising to new life.

All **Thank you for the wine, living Lord.**

Participation

It goes without saying that if children are present at services, they need to be able to participate in order to stay connected. Children should be encouraged to assist by taking part in the service, doing prayers or readings, carrying forward the elements to the table and joining in with prayers and actions.

Make more

This is a prayer that the whole congregation could say together. It would be easier for younger children if each line were repeated.

All **Make more of us, as we share this bread.**
Make more of our understanding of Jesus and his sacrifice.
Make more of us, as we share this wine.
Make more of our understanding of all that Jesus did.
Make more of us, as we share this special meal.
Make more of our worship at this time.
Make more of us, as we end our time of remembering.
Make more of our lives from this time on.

5 Thanking God for his goodness

We are grateful

Leader We are grateful for the meal we can share.

All **Thank you for the gift of life, and the joy of sharing.**

Leader We are grateful for the offering that Jesus made.

All **Thank you for the gift of life, and the joy following.**

Leader We are grateful for the bread and wine, and all that it means.

All **Thank you for the gift of life, and the joy of remembering.**

Leader We are grateful for the hope that the risen Jesus gives us.

All **Thank you for the gift of life, and the joy of hope.**

Leader We are grateful for the Holy Spirit working in our lives.

All **Thank you for the gift of life, and the joy of growing in God.**

Wondering about the future

Ask these 'wondering' questions, allowing a short time after each for the people to think them through and respond for themselves.

Leader I wonder what you will remember about this service.

Leader I wonder what you will remember of the prayers and words we have said.

Leader I wonder what you will remember about the bread and wine.

Leader I wonder what the suffering that Jesus went through means to your life.

Leader I wonder what difference it will make after this time together.

Speak it out

Invite the people to think of one or two things they are really grateful for. It may help to prompt them with suggestions such as family, home, friends, food, and love. As you say 'Generous God, we thank you for . . .', invite everyone to speak out the things they are thankful for. Some will find this easy to do, others will prefer to be quiet!

Thank you, our God

Devise simple actions for the response, 'Thank you, our God'.

All **Thank you, our God**

Leader for everything you have given us.

All **Thank you, our God**

Leader for being part of the special meal.

All **Thank you, our God**

Leader for Jesus and his great love for all of us.

All **Thank you, our God**

Leader for all we have shared today.

All **Thank you, our God**

Leader for our future today, tomorrow and onwards.

Go with us

Leader As we remember what we have learned,

All **creator and Lord, go with us.**

Leader As we think of the bread and wine,

All **creator and Lord, go with us.**

Leader As we remember Jesus alive again,

All **creator and Lord, go with us.**

Leader As we go on to change and to grow,

All **creator and Lord, go with us.**

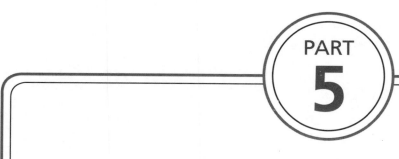

PART 5

Carrying on

Teaching, fellowship and the breaking of bread

The impact of admission to communion on children's discipleship

Steve Dixon

Those who welcomed [Peter's] message were baptized . . . They devoted themselves to the apostles' teaching and fellowship, to the breaking of bread and the prayers.

(Acts 2.41–42)

Introduction

What is the impact on children's discipleship of receiving communion before confirmation and being part of a church community that welcomes baptized children as communicants? To offer a response, this chapter considers both theory and the reflections of children who have been receiving for a number of years, and suggests some implications for those working with children and for the whole Christian community.

1 Discipleship in theory

This section suggests an understanding of discipleship as teaching, fellowship and breaking bread. It then considers aspects of admission to communion that have the potential to enrich children's experience in these areas and so foster their discipleship.

'We none of us are members because we have attained a certain standard of goodness, but rather because, in this matter, we still are humble learners in the school of Christ.'[1] These words of Edgar Dunstan remind us that although 'disciple' indicates a learner, in the Christian context learning is not a prelude to achieving a standard of competence that qualifies us to join the community of faith. Instead, the qualification for membership is *being* a learner: to cease learning is to cease belonging.

But what is the 'school of Christ' like? Jesus' first disciples were continually on the move, so active and varied *teaching* is expected. Those first pupils (especially Peter) also indicate it is messy[2] and difficult to assess[3] – not a steady progress towards a final graduation into 'real life'. It actually *is* the life of faith. Christ's school is also a learning community – a *fellowship*. Jesus called individuals to be part of a diverse group including families, men and women, young and old. And the class always had Jesus at the centre, first in his own flesh, then the bread and wine of remembrance. In the *breaking of bread* they became the body of Christ. The fourth Gospel records that mutual love was the sign by which people would know members of the school of Christ (John 13.35). If membership of the school is diverse, its members will have diverse spiritual, educational and faith development needs, and meeting them will be an indication of the love that signals discipleship.

Perhaps, reflecting the community that gathered at the first Pentecost, we can say that discipleship is characterized by **teaching**, **fellowship** and **breaking of bread** (Acts 2.41–42). The teaching will be an *ongoing* process, *varied* in style to reflect the way of Jesus and the *diversity* of the fellowship; and the fellowship will be *Christ-centred*, exemplified in the breaking of bread.

It is tempting to associate teaching, fellowship and breaking bread with the three Bs – believing, belonging and behaving.[4] However, the messiness of discipleship is indicated by the ongoing debate over the order in which the Bs occur. The elements I have identified above are not distinct – each is part of the other two. They do not form a progression but are ever-present dimensions of the disciple's life, and each involves devotion to 'the prayers'.

In the middle of the nineteenth century the American theologian Horace Bushnell listed exclusion from taking communion among discouragements to piety for the young.[5] How much more might that be true today when children are used to inclusion in everything from planning a holiday to interviewing a prospective head teacher? When those with reservations about children receiving communion query whether they will understand what they are doing, the response is often made that they will certainly understand the rejection if denied a share in the family meal. Childhood experience is formative and powerful, and such alienation may last a lifetime. If exclusion hinders discipleship, then inclusion of children at communion might be expected to encourage it. Using the characterization of discipleship as a blend of teaching, fellowship and the breaking of bread suggested above, let us now explore how such encouragement could take place through admitting children to communion.

Teaching

A Church of England report on the effects of admitting baptized children to communion claimed that the practice leads to 'earlier and greater understanding'.[6] If so, what are the aspects of the practice that might promote such effective learning in the school of Christ?

A varied learning experience

Jesus provided a varied learning experience, and that is an important characteristic of learning when children are admitted to communion. The General Synod Regulations do not specify a minimum age for admission, and the guidelines issued by my own Diocese of Manchester state that the diocesan children's officer should be consulted if very young children are to be admitted. Whenever this happens, I promote **active learning** – learning about the significance of the sacrament by receiving, over several years. This principle does not apply only to the very young, nor solely to children. Disciples of whatever age learn 'on the job' following a cycle of doing, exploring, reflecting then doing again. The learning is in the doing – the receiving.

We would expect the diverse school of Christ to contain members with a variety of learning styles.[7] Yet the teaching offered to children, particularly in worship contexts, can often be word-dominated and passive. This suits a certain kind of learner, but the active involvement of taking communion, and the drama of enacting the Last Supper, enable a wider range of learners to grow in discipleship. And for those who need to know why they are engaged in a learning activity before they can engage, the preparation for admission to communion provides a practical purpose they may find lacking in other nurture groups.

John Westerhoff proposed four **styles of faith**: 'experienced', 'affiliative', 'searching' and 'owned'.[8] In receiving communion, children are engaged in an experience that has the potential to nurture them in whatever style they are doing their faith, and to offer the possibility of developing a new style. In being welcomed to receive the bread and wine, children *experience* the inclusive love that should characterize the family of faith. In being admitted to the communion of the Church, they are *affiliated* to the body of Christ. And in the quiet of their own hearts and minds as they approach the Lord's table, receive, and return to their seats, they are in a safe place in company with God where they can do the *searching* that will open the possibility of *owning* their faith.

The research of David Csinos has identified four **spirituality styles**: 'word', 'emotion', 'symbol' and 'action'.[9] The teaching that children have traditionally received in Church suits those with *word* spirituality; but to provide a balanced diet for all, the other three styles require feeding. The *emotional* engagement of sharing with the family in the Lord's Supper, and the wordless mystery of its *symbols*, are much needed food for those who cannot live by words alone. And every time we 'walk the walk' to share in communion, proclaiming our support for the inclusivity of Christ's body, then spirituality finds expression through *action* in support of kingdom values.

Discipleship is a continuing journey

Admitting baptized children to communion helps children appreciate discipleship as 'journey'. General Synod Regulations require that any parish admitting children 'has made adequate provision for preparation and continuing nurture in the

Christian life and will encourage any child admitted to Holy Communion . . . to be confirmed at the appropriate time'.[10] Several published resources are available to help parishes fulfil this obligation, and a common feature is that they emphasize the journey of faith. Children are reminded of their baptism, encouraged to view admission to communion as the next important event, and explore confirmation as a possible future milestone in their ongoing journey. That they can receive communion when they still have far to go in their Christian lives demonstrates that discipleship is about travelling rather than arriving, and that 'Eucharist is a meal for the road, not for the homecoming.'[11]

Fellowship

To be a full, communicant member of the Church boosts a child's sense of belonging, but does it also foster an appreciation of the Christian community as diverse and Christ-centred?

Inclusive and diverse fellowship

In the welcome they are given, children receive a lesson by example in the inclusive hospitality that marks discipleship. As they have been welcomed in love, so they can grow in discipleship by learning to extend love to diverse neighbours. A celebration of the all-age diversity in the Christian fellowship is encouraged by the process of admission. The published preparation materials encourage the involvement of parents and carers. Indeed, the Diocese of Manchester guidelines require that attempts be made to involve parents/carers in this way and in ongoing nurture after admission; and that if no parent/carer attends church, an adult sponsor be appointed, following proper safeguarding procedures.[12] The guidelines also ask that other properly appointed adults be involved in the preparation, and the process itself gives opportunities for the congregation to support the children in prayer and receive reports on the preparation. Then on the day of admission the whole church can celebrate, showing the children that the community they are part of truly rejoices in the inclusion of young and old. When young and old receive together it is a powerful symbol of our common status as children before our heavenly parent; and when parents receive beside their children, and children with their siblings, it is a wordless lesson that God is 'the

Father, from whom every family in heaven and on earth is named'.[13]

Discipleship is Christ-centred

In whatever way we understand it, the bread and wine bring Christ into the centre of the Christian community; and to receive the bread and wine after hearing the words of institution is to take Christ into the substance of our lives. To become full participants in communion means that the gathering at the table can take its place at the centre of children's experience of worship, and not as something on the periphery from which they are excluded. For communicant children, therefore, Christ is brought into the centre of their experience of membership in the fellowship of faith.

Breaking of bread

When discussing the place of children in the eucharistic community, the Scriptures in which Jesus places children at the centre of adult disciples or rebukes adults who are trying to keep children away are frequently quoted. However, the Diocese of Southwark, in its resource for exploring the Eucharist with children,[14] highlights the story of the Emmaus road (Luke 24.13–35), which is not about children but the sacrament. In this story, although the expounding of Scripture set the hearts of the travellers ablaze, they only recognized Jesus in the breaking of the bread. We began this chapter by noting the word disciple indicates a learner, but it means far more than simply a pupil. 'Disciple' is an incomplete term until we know *whose* disciple a person is. Discipleship requires relationship and devotion to the teacher,[15] and growth in discipleship requires growth in that devotion. The Emmaus story reminds us that the teacher is truly known in the breaking of the bread.

2 Discipleship in practice

In the first section we explored the *potential* that receiving communion has for fostering children's growth in discipleship, but how does that work in practice? To find out, I talked with two fourteen-year-olds – here under the pseudonyms Kim and Chris – whose church has admitted baptized children to communion before confirmation since 2008.[16] They were among the first group to be admitted and so had been receiving for nearly six years at the time of our conversation. This section continues to use the headings **teaching**, **fellowship** and **breaking of bread** as it considers the impact of admission to communion on these young people's discipleship.

Teaching

Both Kim and Chris had been prepared using one of the most popular published resources,[17] and they both remembered the course. The resource features an activity book, and Kim said enthusiastically that she still had hers. The fact that she had gone on to take communion and become part of the eucharistic community had given an added significance to the learning, making her feel 'There's reasons behind it.'

Learning has continued since admission, and as they talked about receiving they demonstrated responses to the different *learning styles* it offers. They both referred to listening and thinking while ministers were speaking in a communion service, but they also valued movement during the peace and when receiving communion, which they described as doing something 'practical' and 'physical'. Their responses to these two elements of the service, described below, indicate they are learning experiences as well as breaks from passive listening. They also responded to the visual and symbolic aspects of the liturgy of the sacrament. The breaking and receiving of the bread were, for both, moments when they thought about the significance of the actions. Kim explained: 'You think about the meaning of it when you're swallowing it.' Her biological description suggests the power of physicality.

As they went on to discuss their thoughts and feelings on receiving, they demonstrated how symbolism and physical involvement combined with more formal instruction to encourage personal exploration and meaning-making:

Kim   It's very symbolic. It reminds you of the Last Supper and stuff that happened.

Chris   When they're snapping the bread it makes me think of when Jesus is on the cross – I don't know why, it just does. 'Cos you're taking it apart.

Kim   It's like sharing, isn't it? It looks like, like sharing communion.

Chris   Yeah, it's like splitting it up, it makes it look like it's for everyone, and that we're all part of one.

Kim   It is – we're all drinking from the same cup . . .

Chris   That's the idea, isn't it?

Kim   It's just like from one body.

Of Csinos's four *spirituality styles*, 'word' and 'action' are indicated in the young people's responses above. In addition, Chris's comment, 'I don't know why, it just does', is an indication of spiritual engagement beyond words – the style that finds expression in 'symbol', if at all. The symbolism in a eucharistic service was referred to frequently by both and led to their considering the merits of real or wafer bread. Chris preferred the former, but Kim suggested the latter gave a better sense of symbolism and the specialness of communion.

Spirituality in the 'emotion' style was also evident. Both young people appreciated the peace and the opportunity it gave for sharing a special greeting with others. Kim identified 'Peace be with you' as one of the phrases in the liturgy that she particularly liked and, reflecting on the exchange of the peace, remarked, 'I think it makes *you* feel better. I think it makes *other people* feel better.' And when Chris suggested that older people, who can't get up, appreciate receiving the peace, she added, 'And then *you* feel better, yourself, for doing that.' Thinking about returning to her seat after receiving, Kim stated, 'You feel more calm, I think, when you've taken communion . . . You feel calmer in yourself.'

The sense of belonging associated with Westerhoff's 'affiliative' *style of faith* is central to the question of children's full participation in communion. The importance of sharing bread and wine for their sense of belonging was strikingly demonstrated when Kim and Chris described their experiences of receiving and being denied communion. This was Chris's description of the difference he felt when he was admitted to communion:

> When you feel like everyone does it, you're part of it, but when you didn't do it before, you felt like you weren't actually part of it and you were just more an outsider that came occasionally.

When they were younger communicants, both Chris and Kim had experienced being refused communion at churches where they were not known.[18] Chris described being 'horrified' when he was 'skipped' at the distribution and felt he was 'missing out' when he couldn't complete his communion. Kim affirmed his feelings as he continued:

Chris   You just want to be part of it don't you, and you've been at the build up, you're expecting to get it, you've kind of prepared yourself for that and then you don't. And [you feel] a bit . . .

Kim   . . . down . . .

Chris   . . . anticlimax.

It is to be hoped that a settled sense of belonging will give Kim and Chris a secure place to develop the 'questioning' that will nurture their spiritual development. Their reflections on their early experience of receiving gave an indication of the importance feeling at ease in the community has for learning. Both Kim and Chris had initially felt anxious about practicalities – not being able to reach the rail, not receiving correctly or choking on the wafer, and the problem of who leaves first in a line of communicants. They both said that these things had proved distractions to thought and prayer at the moment of reception. However, Kim now feels 'a lot more comfortable going up as a community to receive', and the hope is that her sense of normality in being a communicant will enable her to feed more richly on the sacrament as she journeys on in her discipleship.

The sense of ongoing journey was evident in the conversation. Both young people felt that becoming communicant had been a sign of 'growing up' for them, but this was not just about life stages. Chris felt he was 'taking a step further into Christianity'; and for Kim the importance was not simply that she was no longer regarded as a child, but that people saw her as someone who 'knew what was happening'. Chris acknowledged during preparation that there had been an excited anticipation of receiving, and part of him had wanted to get the course over so he could do this; but he also reflected that taking bread and wine was not the end of the story – his understanding as a communicant had developed over subsequent years.

Chris and Kim showed different approaches to the place of confirmation in their journey. Chris conceded, 'I probably don't know all there is to know', but he was comfortable with that and it had not prevented him deciding to be confirmed. Kim, however, had taken what she described as 'quite a hard decision' not to be confirmed for the time being. She explained:

> I was still discovering things. If I still didn't understand it fully, I just didn't want to go making that commitment when I still didn't understand it myself fully. I thought I'd rather wait a couple more years until I was ready to.

Fellowship

The most striking feature of the conversation was the central importance Chris and Kim gave to community in their reflections on receiving communion. We have already seen that the breaking of the bread was not just about them receiving – they valued the fact that it was shared for all; and Kim suggested 'sharing like one body' as words from the liturgy that stuck in her mind.[19] The young people developed their reflections on this phrase into a definition of its significance:

Chris   I think the main part of it is, is that we are all one. We worship one God. We are all followers of him. We're all from the same family.

Kim   We all join together to do this – communion! It's a community.

Chris noted that the Church welcomed anyone and everyone, and both valued the diversity of the community to which they felt themselves to belong. Kim had enjoyed having her family with her when she first received and, discussing the diversity of ages in the congregation, she linked this to communion by observing, 'You're all going together to do something.' Chris was emphatic that he was talking about all ages, from toddlers to the aged, when he described silently greeting people with a smile in the queue to the altar and back.

Although they had both had the distressing experience of being refused communion in churches other than their own, they had also had the pleasure of receiving alongside 'strangers' in other churches, and this had given them a sense of the wider diversity of their faith community. Kim had received communion in America and described how:

> It was good to be part of a different community . . . people I'd no idea who they were . . . but still felt part of a community, you know. I didn't really know anyone [but] still felt part of a group doing it together.

Chris continued this reflection by suggesting:

> Even though you don't know one another, you don't know the people that you're doing it with, you still have a kind of almost a sense that you *do* know that person — you know a part about that person because *they're* taking communion and they're . . . part of the family of God.

When reflecting on being 'sent out into the world' after communion, both thought that being part of the Church community helped them avoid peer pressure to engage in questionable behaviour. For Chris, 'There's something that holds you back . . . There's something that says no, that's not right.' And Kim linked this directly with being a communicant, explaining:

> When you've received as a community, like communion and stuff, it makes you feel part of something completely different. You don't want to be part of something that's like wrong, feels in a sense wrong.

And that receiving community is *Christ centred*. Chris expressed his sense of the presence of Jesus in the sacrament as follows:

> It's a bit odd, you drinking the blood of Christ. I mean you wouldn't literally drink anyone's blood, would you? It's weird, but it's the symbolism of the Christ that's the important thing and also that it's always there. I mean obviously they make the bread and you can buy the wine and water it down, but — it's always there — it never runs out, like the spirit of Jesus never runs out. It's always there.

Kim agreed: 'He's always there.'

Breaking of bread

It was clear from our conversation that these two young communicants felt themselves to be fully

signed up members of the school of Christ — disciples. But how much of their growth in discipleship has been helped by becoming communicants and how much might have happened simply through belonging to a 'child friendly' church community?

The following aspects of the young people's responses arose directly from receiving:

- The course they undertook had extra value in being a preparation to receive.
- The act of reception was a stimulus for reflection.
- The moment after receiving provided a special time of inner calm.
- Receiving gave a potent sense of inclusion, and being denied communion produced a powerful feeling of exclusion.
- Receiving was perceived as 'taking a step further' in the faith.
- 'Sharing like one body' was seen as a mark of community.
- Membership of the eucharistic fellowship gave strength to resist incorporation into unhealthy 'communities'.
- The inexhaustible presence of Christ was discerned in bread and wine.

A final, and potent indication of the importance communion has for these young people's discipleship is the value they themselves place on it. They both lead 'busy lives' and are not able to take communion every time, or even most times it is celebrated. However, they both expressed regret about this. Chris said that when he is able to attend church he enjoys it, 'especially the communion bit'. Kim was able to state exactly when she had last received communion, and when she hasn't done so for some time she feels 'like I missed out'.

To enable these and other youngsters in a similar situation to maintain contact with their church, a fortnightly Sunday evening group has been arranged. Both Chris and Kim enquired about the possibility of having communion as part of this group. Since the group's activities include a large social element, the request that time be set aside for the breaking of bread is a strong indication of the value these young people place on communion.

3 Discipleship for all

So far we have explored the impact of admission to communion on children, but what about its effect on the whole congregation?

Horace Bushnell assessed 'qualification' for providing Christian nurture to children by negatives. One consideration was that anyone who resented the disruption to their previous way of life caused by caring for children was not qualified to offer them Christian nurture.[20] Having children necessitates change, and this is as true for a church as for any other family. It's part of the deal. But it is also good news. For many adults, nurturing children is an enriching experience. As it turns their world upside down it teaches them about life and love – and about God: things they would not otherwise have experienced.[21] The same can be said of a church: if it is not prepared to have its world permanently changed by children, it is not qualified to nurture them in the faith; and moreover, it will miss the opportunity to grow in love and discipleship.

Inspired by the way Jesus asked his first disciples to consider the nature of the Kingdom by placing a child in their midst (see Matthew 18.1–5; Mark 9.33–37; Luke 9.46–48), the Child Theology Movement has made a practice of considering theological questions by imagining a child at their centre.[22] The admission of children to communion goes one better than imagining: it emulates the practice of Jesus by placing real children in the midst of adult disciples as they share bread and wine and become the body of Christ so that the Church can re-envision its theology. In this way, not only can admission foster children's growth in discipleship but the transformation of congregational life can also offer opportunities for adults to develop in their faith.

Whenever children are being prepared for admission, there are opportunities for their work to be shared with and celebrated by all, and some churches prepare children through an annual programme of teaching for the whole congregation on the Eucharist. The preparation of children for communion also raises the issue of 'understanding', inviting a congregation to broaden its view of what this means and to redress an over-emphasis on the cerebral. Ultimately the question of 'qualification' to receive communion arises. As the Knaresborough Report put it, admission of children to communion 'proclaims in a concrete way that belonging to Christ's body is a gift of grace':[23] in recognizing the right of baptized children to membership, a congregation can grow in its understanding of what it means to be the body of Christ. In learning to be generous in its welcome, and caring towards those with least power, a congregation can grow more fully into the stature of the body it proclaims itself to be. When Jesus placed a child in the midst of the adult disciples, he told them they must change and become like children to enter the kingdom. To welcome children at the Lord's table is an ever-present reminder that before God people of all ages are children, privileged by grace to share in the bread of life and cup of salvation.

As a diocesan children's ministry adviser, I find that discussing admission provides an opportunity for adult disciples to consider what they understand by communion and membership of the body of Christ in a depth and with a concentration that they may not have done for years. They are also invited to consider whether the practice of admission to communion on the strength of baptism enables both baptism and confirmation to be taken more seriously than they may have been before: the former as a complete rite of entry into the Christian community; and the latter as a commitment to adult responsibility within that community, which – as the example of Kim and Chris demonstrated – may occur sooner or later in a person's life, as the Spirit directs. I am always delighted when asked to share in a church's deliberations on admission to communion as, whatever the outcome, the process leads to prayerful theological engagement and offers the opportunity for adults to grow in discipleship. I also find it is an issue that can stimulate growth through a changed perspective. One adult member of a church considering the practice opposed it on the basis that children should not be given everything at once but should learn to wait. However, after a number of discussions, she came to a different view. 'I still think children shouldn't get everything at once,' she told me, 'but this is too important to make them wait.'

In addition to growth for existing members, the admission of children to communion has had an unexpected missional effect. Parents of children preparing for admission are often not confirmed, regular churchgoers or even baptized. Through engagement in the preparation programmes, many of these unchurched parents/carers become engaged in considering the faith, start attending church and even present themselves for baptism and/or confirmation.

Conclusion: implications for practice

The foregoing consideration of the effects of admitting children to communion on the strength of their baptism has implications for those churches that adopt the practice.

They should expect a growth in children's discipleship and maximize opportunities for realizing the potential provided by children receiving communion. They should also expect congregational life to be changed and enriched. These expectations might be reflected in:

- valuing and promoting the diversity of experience provided by communion as a way of meeting children's varied spiritual, developmental and educational needs;

- incorporating the active, participatory, multi-sensory and reflective characteristics of receiving communion into the rest of worship, thus enriching the experience of all ages;

- celebrating the body of Christ – its diversity and its welcoming, inclusive nature;

- encouraging children to receive communion in varied settings beyond their own church, and facilitating this broadening of their experience;

- providing other opportunities, apart from the main parish Eucharist, for children to receive communion within their own church setting;

- promoting preparation for admission as a family activity and encouraging parents to use it as an opportunity to reflect on their own faith and ask questions;

- providing opportunities for young communicants to discuss and reflect on their continuing experience of receiving, within their families and in their nurture groups;

- facilitating whole-congregation interest in and support of the candidates being prepared for admission and a whole-congregation approach to exploring the Eucharist;

- exploring as a congregation the importance that admission gives to baptism as a complete rite of entry, to confirmation as a mature act of commitment, and to the Scriptures in which Jesus draws children close to him;

- expecting that, thanks to the presence of children at the Lord's table, adults will grow in their discipleship, and congregational life will be transformed.

A case study of the impact on one church of admitting children to communion

Nick Harding

This case study is drawn from a real church but all names and identities have been changed. All comments and observations come from church members, leaders and children from 'All Saints Church' and others at a similar stage in the process of admitting children to Holy Communion.

On a May Sunday morning All Saints Church was full, with a happy congregation and a sense of celebration. All Saints is in an urban area of a city, and most of the congregation live within walking distance. The service this morning is all-age, and includes the welcoming of another 12 children and young people to receive communion for the first time. The church has been welcoming children in this way for the past five years, and has seen numbers grow within their children's and youth work; it is proving to be a magnet for local families. Despite hard work on the part of Sharon, the vicar, the church has lost a few older people from the main Sunday service because they don't like the noise children and families make, but she considers this a sad but necessary price to pay.

The service was special according to the children who received communion for the first time. The sense of celebration was tempered with a reminder that the Eucharist is an important and meaningful part of the Christian life and worship, and should not be taken lightly or without reverence.

The church has seen admitting children to communion before confirmation as a natural step in helping children and young people feel welcome, and very much a part of the church community. Parents and carers have relished the opportunity to see their children grow, and have learned much

about their own children's faith and maturity along the way.

In churches such as All Saints the church leadership have a view on what it does to the whole church community when children receive. Most church leaders are unifiers, and see the Eucharist as one of the key moments when the whole church community gathers and takes part as one in a special moment.

> It's really important that they can join in if they want to. None of us fully understand but we can all enjoy the joy of joining together as one family and celebrating this special meal together.

Church leaders see the benefits of the whole family having the opportunity to share together in the special meal. Some recognize that adults as well as the children concerned learn a lot from one another, and understand more fully that we are all on a spiritual journey, no matter how old or young we are.

> It has been a real treat to see how some of the reluctant congregation members have taken the children under their wings, and have helped to break down the generational barriers.

> It helps to make the whole church feel inclusive in a better way, to be the people of God properly and helps the children to think about their faith in a much deeper way, giving them a sense of belonging to their faith.

There are some clergy who still struggle with the idea of children having to go through 'preparation', and who would much prefer to have an 'open table' for all, regardless of age.

> If I personally give communion to all children, then I could be officially disciplined and sacked! I would love to offer it to anyone, but can't.

> I don't get all this preparation stuff – I don't stand on the chancel steps and challenge the adults about what they understand and how they were prepared to receive, so . . . why should I do that for children?

> Some people really want their family to receive communion, and are frustrated that the children have to . . . wait for others, and do a course.

Children receiving communion before confirmation does raise some issues about what confirmation is about, and what it is for. There are many complicated reasons why young people are not being confirmed in the numbers they once were, although one of the main reasons is that there are not as many young people in our churches. There are also postmodern issues about what 'membership' means to young people. If they receive communion early, what is the motivation for them to be confirmed? This again raises the issue of where children receiving and where young people being confirmed fits in the church's overall plan and strategy to care for and nurture the young.

> I always feel the Church has made a formality over confirmation. I can't see anything about it in the Bible. If someone feels they want to obey the Lord's commandment to remember him while eating and drinking, why can't they be allowed to do it, regardless of their age?

> For me taking communion is a smaller step for a child than choosing to commit to the Christian faith (in confirmation and so on), which is a long-term decision on how they will live for many years. I don't think a child can make a meaningful decision on such a long-term matter until after puberty, when confirmation really means something.

> It is an opportunity for them, at the right stage and age, to make their own declaration of faith

before taking the further step of confirmation later on.

There are, of course, ways to make a lot of both children receiving communion for the first time, and those who have just been confirmed. Here's a comment from one church:

> The children received their first communion together with the people who had been confirmed the week previously. [It was] a very special day for all of them at which [the children] received their certificates for completing the course.

The reality that some parents choose to allow their children to receive and some do not tends to be a cause of frustration rather than division. Children go to the rail alongside one another and some put their hands out, while others do not. In the many hundreds of churches across the country who have made progress on this there are few reports of marked division, or children being particularly concerned or jealous of others. But some children's leaders and parents are aware that it could cause an unhelpful sense of separation between peers:

> It seems sad to me that some parents choose to exclude their children from this special thing. The children look sad too . . . like they are so near and yet so far from something real and good for them.

> I don't know whether my daughter feels left out or not – it's not something we talk about. I don't really want to discuss it anyway, because I'm not sure I could explain my thinking to her.

The behaviour of children at communion, and their level of understanding of what they are doing and what it all means, are issues that become less apparent as children regularly receive alongside their peers, families and church family. What we have to remember is that children will be children, and while they may be noisy or disruptive at times, they can also take things very seriously and have developed a profound and moving understanding of the deeper spiritual things. But receiving communion doesn't mean they will suddenly change into perfect, subservient 'angels' who have lost their childlike energy and enthusiasm for being who they are – and nor should they!

> I notice that it's about belonging for our children – they are generally very well behaved – they sense it is important and they want to belong and I want them all to know they are welcome and that they belong.

> A child who has some understanding of what it is about (who of us has complete understanding?), is able to make an informed and meaningful choice. Some will just follow habit, but that is a feature of us all and adults aren't excluded on this basis.

> It has shown me how much knowledge, faith and understanding they have. They feel a strong identity with the church and faith and this will help their sense of belonging.

> People talk about understanding but I find that my daughters have always known this is important and want to be part of it. We have a number of adults with learning disability who belong to our church and take communion. They understand this is important as well and know that they are included.

> I'm happy in that children don't feel segregated from the 'grown ups' doing some 'mysterious thing' and that they feel part of the service.

> There are no riots, children don't mess around. In fact, they seem to take it all more seriously than some of the adults!

Parents who have chosen to allow this step for their children are usually very positive, and in some cases it has made a significant difference to the whole family as they have discussed the issues in preparation and are regularly able to share in the feast together. Many parents have reported that they have been surprised at their own child's spiritual understanding and depth through their participation in communion.

> We have only been attending this church for almost 18 months but the difference it's made to us all as a family to share in communion has been amazing. My youngest especially has made steps in his confidence (still a long way to go!) and has told us that he feels so safe there – you can't ask for more than that!

> I think I have become more passionate about this as I go along. As a mum I cannot refuse my daughters something that does us all good spiritually.

> I feel confident taking part in family communion has increased her inclusion and spiritual awareness.

> It is special to see them on either side of me, doing the same as me. That's what family is about – us as a family, in the family of the church.

> My children feel a strong identity with the church and faith and this will help their sense of belonging.

Conclusion

Most children see taking communion as a normal and important part of what they do in church, and enjoy being able to share with the adults. For some this is partly about privilege, but for most it is a significant and deep moment in their spiritual journey. So as we consider the benefits of joining in, it seems right to leave the last word to some children:

> It means I can share with people Jesus' body and blood to make sure that I always remember that Jesus died for us.

> I look forward to taking communion with my mum, and being the same as everyone else.

> I enjoy joining in, and I know it's what Jesus did with his friends. I don't like the taste of the wine though!

Beyond the church: ideas and resources for school Eucharists

Nick Harding and Sandra Millar

One of the steps a church might like to take is to work with the local church school to develop a school Eucharist, something that is already embedded practice in some dioceses. For some schools this might be a very formal occasion, marking the end or beginning of term, perhaps taking place in the church. However, there is an opportunity to develop something fresh. It is possible to turn the school hall into a creative worship space and give every child the opportunity to discover what communion means, and for some of them to share it for themselves.

> As the priest for this community, I see it as essential that children are present when the Eucharist is shared. It is part of the rhythm of life for my parish.
>
> A parish priest

Creative ideas for school Eucharists

One of the ways to explore the meaning of Eucharist with the whole school is through a series of interactive stations. This approach to faith exploration is used very successfully through a range of resources published by Jumping Fish and Prayer Stations in Schools.[1]

> We learned all about it by doing activities around the dining room. I think this helped me a bit.
>
> A school pupil

This approach divides classes into small groups and then enables each small group to work through a different aspect of the story or theme being explored in an accessible and interactive way, which gives lots of time for reflection and questions. The stations are prepared and presented by the local church, which helps to develop the school–church relationship and also gives children an experience that goes beyond the educational, giving them space to wonder and respond in their own way.

It is possible to explore the Eucharist in a similar way, setting up a series of stations. This can be used not just for the school to think about what Eucharist means but also by the church to help those who want to take communion for the first time to prepare. In that instance, families could be invited back for one evening in the week and given the opportunity to explore the stations with the clergy and to use this as a basis for being admitted to communion, which then happens at the first school Eucharist. It is worth remembering that there are pastoral challenges and protocols here, and children can be admitted to communion only through a parish church. However, if the school is working with the vicar then this could happen in the school eucharistic context. The risk remains that, if children are not clearly connected in to the worshipping community of the church, they may drift off.

> I decided to encourage our PCC to support this a number of years ago now with a view to inviting members of the Year 6 class at the school to prepare to be admitted to communion. This was after my experiences with confirmation and the fact that once confirmed many of the children did not keep in touch with the church. If I am being honest the same has happened with admission to communion, although a few do come, but on a less frequent basis.
>
> A parish priest

In schools where having a Eucharist in school is already established, it can have a major impact on the lives of both children and staff. It becomes a marker for transitions and a place of belonging, even for those who do not receive communion. In one school where a termly Eucharist has been established for a number of years, some Year 6 children spoke freely about their experiences. All of them were very clear that it helped them to feel a strong sense of community, gave them confidence and courage as they faced the next stage in their journey and helped children at every stage to grow in their understanding of faith. One young boy, who did not himself receive communion, said:

> It doesn't matter whether you have the bread, or whether you don't have the bread. The point is that the presence of Jesus blesses everyone.
>
> A school pupil

His confidence in the place of the school Eucharist in his experience of school was memorable. It was also interesting hearing a newly qualified teacher talking about joining a school that had a regular communion service. She commented that nothing in her training had suggested such a possibility to her, but having come to the school, she had found it an important and special space in the term. It allowed her some space for reflection, helped her to see the school as a whole and to appreciate its distinctive qualities. Although she did not define herself as a believer, the Eucharist had made a big impact on her thinking.

Of course, many schools choose not to proceed with Holy Communion for their own well-considered reasons. One head teacher comments:

> We thought about this as a school, but as most of the children wouldn't be able to receive we decided not to make it a regular thing. School is all about children, and we want everything we do to be as inclusive as possible.

Where a school is holding a Eucharist regularly, there are lots of opportunities for children to be involved in leading and preparing, many of which can be incorporated into classroom activities. It is an opportunity to present worship in an engaging, multi-sensory, accessible way, suited to the age and stage of the children. And there is no doubt that for the younger children, the most important and influential role models are those in Years 5 and 6. Seeing them leading worship, planning and preparing, sharing faith and engaging with the lived experience of school, can make a big impact.

Children might be involved in writing responsive prayers to use in the opening section, or in designing a corporate praise shout. For the confession, in one school the children made a short film themselves, where they set up scenes, acted by themselves, showing the kind of things that children do wrong in a typical school day (fighting, being unkind, not sharing, answering back), and then wrote their own prayers of repentance – an opportunity for saying sorry – to go alongside. There are lots of other creative ways of asking for God's forgiveness, and almost any class could prepare this kind of activity.

There are many ways to present the stories from the Bible, apart from just reading them. A class could prepare a drama or involve everyone in portraying a story. One Year 1 group acted out the story of the lost sheep, with almost everyone in the class wearing sheep masks they had made earlier. Drama, dance, mime and song could all be used.

There may be time for a short space for wondering together about the story, asking the children to think about its meaning or purpose for them. Or it may be that they have already done this work earlier in the classroom and will bring the fruits of their reflections to the Eucharist. If Godly Play is being used in school,[2] then a story could be told and explored and responded to in every class before the Eucharist takes place.

> I like it when we have to be quiet and think for ourselves – I like the peace, and the thoughts that pop into my mind.
>
> A school pupil

It is good to involve children in developing and leading prayers and it is possible to be a lot more creative than simply standing a line of children in a row and getting them to read one line each. Working with a class to develop intercessions for the things that matter to their school and their community can lead to some imaginative prayers. One school used photos and film clips from an overseas partner school as a trigger for prayer.

Another Year 6 group did a survey in the school to find out where children had relatives across the country, and the world, then presented a map with lots of hearts on it to pray for those places.

Children can also be involved in writing songs, playing music, helping to set up the worship space and taking part in various ways, just as they would in church.

All children should come forward together, whether they receive bread or wine or not, and be aware that God's love and blessing is for all.

One school, familiar with holding a Eucharist, had pushed into a new direction by holding a Eucharist at the end of the school fete, an optional time for families. The head teacher was delighted that a significant number stayed to take part, so that the whole school family could express their faith together.

Issues and challenges

It is now recognized that school Eucharists can be a mission opportunity in some schools and situations. Children and staff together, along with parents and others from the school community, can share not only in worship but in the special meal that unites believers across the world. But there are a number of pastoral and practical issues to be considered too in order for the school to move forward with this smoothly and fairly. We will consider these here.

Younger pupils

School Eucharists can be appropriate in primary schools with younger children if some of the children are regular worshippers and receive communion in the parish church, or their own church if they don't attend the local one. There needs to be careful pastoral work with the church and parents to ensure that they are happy for children to receive, and children are suitably prepared. Even those children who do not receive communion should have some teaching about what is happening, and the option to be admitted when they and their parents or carers think it is time.

Inclusion

One of the less attractive scenarios is when a primary school has a regular Eucharist but only the adults there take part. This does, of course, mirror what happens in many churches, but is much more distinct and noticeable when by far the majority of people there are children who can't take part. Rather than being a celebration of all worshippers, this accentuates the exclusion rather than inclusion of most in the school community.

Liturgy

In 2012 the Church of England introduced two new Eucharistic Prayers that are especially suitable for use when the majority of people present are children, and are the most appropriate prayers for use in schools.[3] The responses include opportunities for children to ask questions, and to change their volume with repetition. This more creative approach will engage children well in a school, and provides better opportunities for participation. There is also room in these new prayers for children and young people to create their own words and prefaces, which provides a good opportunity to teach about the significance of the feast.

Secondary schools

School Eucharists in church secondary schools are common, and in many are a key feature of the school's Christian distinctiveness and worshipping life. However, the reality that the pupils generally come from a wide area creates pastoral challenges for the school.

Churches in the area

Local clergy who are in the catchment area of the school need to discuss and agree a policy and approach to children receiving communion at school. There needs to be an agreement about who is responsible for preparing the young people to receive communion. The pupils could follow a communion preparation course in the school, or potentially the local parish churches could work together. It may work out best for the young people to be prepared in their own individual churches.

Ecumenical challenges

There needs to be some consideration about the ecumenical nature of school worship. Most church schools have pupils from other Christian denominations, and each of those may have a slightly different view about what communion is and who should or should not be allowed to receive. It may be that some of those church leaders are willing to discuss the issue or even make exceptions to their normal attitudes and policy for their young people who attend the school. On the other hand, an 'open table' in school, where anyone is welcome to receive, could undermine other churches and be pastorally insensitive.

Leaders and assistants

At the time of writing, the General Synod of the Church of England has yet to approve guidelines to allow people who are not confirmed but are regular communicants to assist in the administration of communion. If it does approve such guidelines, those communicants would be deemed suitable for such a role, and the bishop, if he or she chooses, could delegate the giving of permission to a parish priest. In a secondary school context this would mean that young people who are regular communicants

would have the permission of their own parish priest in order to assist with the communion in school. It might be possible for the priest of the parish where the school is, or the school chaplain, to give this permission, but it would always have to be done with reference to the home church leader.

Whole school community

The importance and significance of the Eucharist in a community is diluted if the whole community is not present. Where possible whole year groups or whole schools, including staff, should be present in order for the worshipping community to share in the special meal. In some schools where space is limited attendance at Holy Communion is optional, but that may not be the ideal and only partially helps in reinforcing the Christian ethos of the school.

Notes

Introduction

1   Rebecca Nye, *Children's Spirituality: What it is and Why it Matters* (London: Church House Publishing, 2009).

2   *Common Worship: Additional Eucharistic Prayers: With Guidance on Celebrating the Eucharist with Children* (London: Church House Publishing, 2012).

1 Why it matters

1   *Christian Initiation: Birth and Growth in the Christian Society – The Report of the Commission on Christian Initiation* (London: Church Information Office, 1971). In the quotations from this report (taken from its paragraphs 71, 108, 119–121), instances of emphasis/italics are in the original.

2 Children and Holy Communion

1   *Christian Initiation: Birth and Growth in the Christian Society – The Report of the Commission on Christian Initiation* (London: Church Information Office, 1971).

2   *Communion Before Confirmation?* (The Knaresborough Report) (London: CIO Publishing, 1985).

3   Brian Kay, Jan Greenough and John Gay, *Communion before Confirmation: A Report on the Survey conducted by Culham College Institute* (Abingdon: Culham College Institute, 1993).

4   *On the Way: Towards an Integrated Approach to Christian Initiation* (London: Church House Publishing, 1995).

4 Taking the next steps

1   Church Growth Research Programme, *From Anecdote to Evidence: Findings from the Church Growth Research Programme 2011–2013* – <www.churchgrowthresearch.org.uk/UserFiles/File/Reports/FromAnecdoteToEvidence1.0.pdf>.

5 A 'getting ready' story

1   The quotes in this chapter are not verbatim but are taken from notes made at various events.

6 Feasting together

1   Sandra Millar, *Worship Together: Creating All-age Services that Work* (London: SPCK, 2012), p. 91.

2   *New Patterns for Worship* (London: Church House Publishing, 2002), B77, p. 96 (also <www.churchofengland.org/prayer-worship/worship/texts/newpatterns/contents/sectionb.aspx>).

3   *Common Worship: Christian Initiation* (London: Church House Publishing, 2006), p. 77.

7 Including children in eucharistic worship

1   Michele Guinness, *The Heavenly Party: Recover the Fun: Life-changing Celebrations for Home and Community* (Oxford: Monarch Books, 2007).

2   Andy Bates, 'Dinner Time: Should Families Eat Together Every Night?', 10 February 2014, <www.bbc.co.uk/food/0/26068619>.

3   Sam McBratney, illus. Anita Jeram, *Guess How Much I Love You* (London: Walker Books, 1994).

4   See <www.churchofengland.org/prayer-worship/worship/texts/additional-eucharistic-prayers.aspx>.

8 An outline service for admitting children to Holy Communion

1   Antonia White, *Frost in May* (London: Desmond Harmsworth, 1933; repr. London: Virago, 1978), p. 83.

2   Section 'Admission of the Baptized to Communion' in chapter 'Rites of Affirmation: Approaching Baptism' – *Common Worship: Christian Initiation* (London: Church House Publishing, 2006), pp. 188–92. Also at <www.churchofengland.org/prayer-worship/worship/texts/christian-initiation-pdf-contents.aspx>.

3   See <www.churchofengland.org/prayer-worship/worship/texts/the-calendar/lect/lectrules.aspx>, rule 7.

4   *New Patterns for Worship* (London: Church House Publishing, 2002), E6, p. 163.

5   An age-appropriate Bible is a good idea, and Admission to Communion certificates are available from Church House Publishing and others.

6   The St Hilda Community, *The New Women Included: A Book of Services and Prayers* (London: SPCK, 1996), p. 55.

7 *Common Worship: Christian Initiation*, p. 190.

8 See *Common Worship: Services and Prayers for the Church of England* (London: Church House Publishing, 2000); *Common Worship*, Order One, pp. 194–5.

9 *New Patterns for Worship*, p. 297.

9 Additional prayers

1 *Common Worship: Additional Eucharistic Prayers: With Guidance on Celebrating the Eucharist with Children* (London: Church House Publishing, 2012), and at <www.churchofengland.org/prayer-worship/worship/texts/additional-eucharistic-prayers.aspx>.

10 Teaching, fellowship and the breaking of bread

1 Religious Society of Friends, *Quaker Faith and Practice* (Britain Yearly Meeting, 1995), 11.18.

2 Two recent Messy Church publications offer fresh perspectives on Christian discipleship: George Lings (ed.), *Messy Church Theology* (Abingdon: Bible Reading Fellowship, 2013); Paul Moore, *Making Disciples in Messy Church* (Abingdon: Bible Reading Fellowship, 2013).

3 Although a tool such as the Engel Scale – James F. Engel and Wilbert H. Norton, *What's Gone Wrong with the Harvest?* (Grand Rapids, MI: Zondervan, 1975) – provides key locations in a tour of Christian awareness, the picture it gives of an orderly progression does not always match the vagaries of real spiritual life.

4 Developed from Grace Davie, *Religion in Britain Since 1945: Believing Without Belonging* (Oxford: Blackwell, 1994), and widely used as categories for considering discipleship issues.

5 Horace Bushnell, *Christian Nurture* (New York: Charles Scribner's Sons (1847), 1908), pp. 191–203.

6 Brian Kay, Jan Greenough and John Gay, *Communion before Confirmation: A Report on the Survey conducted by Culham College Institute* (Abingdon: Culham College Institute, 1993), p. 25. The report was drawn from a survey of experiences in dioceses 'experimenting' with the practices, prior to the issuing of General Synod Guidelines.

7 One 'learning style' model I often use identifies: imaginative, analytic, common sense and dynamic learners – Marlene LeFever, *Learning Styles* (London: Kingsway Publications, 1995, 2006). The following also explores the importance of including visual, aural, reading/writing and kinaesthetic approaches – Consultative Group on Ministry Among Children (ed.), *Core Skills for Children's Work: Developing and Extending Key Skills for Children's Ministry* (Abingdon: Bible Reading Fellowship, 2006).

8 John H. Westerhoff III, *Will Our Children Have Faith?* (Harrisburg, PA: Morehouse Publishing, 1976, 2000 and 2012).

9 David M. Csinos, *Children's Ministry that Fits: Beyond One-size-fits all Approaches to Nurturing Children's Spirituality* (Eugene, OR: Wipf & Stock, 2011).

10 Paragraph 5 of Regulations made in June 2006, under paragraph 1(c) of Canon B 15A.

11 Peter Reiss, *Children and Communion* (Cambridge: Grove Books, 1998), p. 9.

12 See <www.manchester.anglican.org/education/children>.

13 *Common Worship*, New Patterns for Worship, 'Creeds and Authorized Affirmations of Faith' (London: Church House Publishing, 2000).

14 Diane Craven and Mark Stafford (eds), *About to Receive: Resources for Exploring the Eucharist* (London: Diocese of Southwark, 2005).

15 See R. S. Rayburn's article on 'Names of Christians' in *The Concise Evangelical Dictionary of Theology* (London: Marshall Pickering, 1991), p. 91.

16 At the time of writing I am conducting further research with a larger number of children of junior school age in Diocese of Manchester parishes. Early data indicates that this younger age group is also growing in learning, sense of fellowship, and relationship with Jesus through the breaking of bread.

17 Margaret Withers, *Welcome to the Lord's Table* (Abingdon: Bible Reading Fellowship, 1999).

18 Such a rejection is in breach of paragraph 10 of the General Synod Regulations. The situations probably arose from mistaken assumptions regarding children's participation, rather than conscious refusal to accept their communicant status.

19 Probably a condensing of the words at the breaking of the bread: 'Though we are many, we are one body, because we all share in one bread.'

20 Bushnell, *Christian Nurture*, pp. 164ff.

21 For a detailed account of this, see Veronica Zundel, *Everything I Know About God I've Learned from Being a Parent* (Abingdon: Bible Reading Fellowship, 2013).

22 See Keith White and Haddon Willmer, *An Introduction to Child Theology* (London: Child Theology Movement, 2006).

23 *Communion Before Confirmation?* (The Knaresborough Report) (London: CIO Publishing, 1985), p. 33.

NOTES TO PAGES 92–94

12 Beyond the church

1   See Jumping Fish, *Experience Easter* and others in the 'Experience' series – <gloucester.anglican.org/schools/jumping-fish-publications>. Prayer Stations in Schools – <www.prayerspacesinschools.com/home> – also have resources in this area.

2   See <www.godlyplay.org.uk>.

3   *Common Worship: Additional Eucharistic Prayers, with Guidance on Celebrating the Eucharist with Children* (London: Church House Publishing, 2012); <www.churchofengland.org/prayer-worship/worship/texts/additional-eucharistic-prayers.aspx>.

Further resources

There is always more to learn, and other resources to help and support work with children and young people on the Eucharist. This list is not exhaustive, but gives some key resources where more information and theory is available.

Caldwell, Elizabeth Francis, *Come Unto Me: Rethinking the Sacraments for Children* (Cleveland, OH: United Church Press, 1996). Good exploration of both baptism and communion, with practical sessions to help parents support their child's spiritual growth.

Lake, Stephen, *Let the Children Come to Communion* (London: SPCK, 2006). Very good history and background to children and communion, with good tips on practicalities and experience from a range of people.

Nye, Rebecca, *Children's Spirituality: What it is and Why it Matters* (London: Church House Publishing, 2009). Essential reading for understanding how children's spirituality and faith grow and are nurtured.

Resources to use with children

Brown, Joan, *Meet Christ with Joy: Preparation for First Communion* (Stowmarket: Kevin Mayhew, 1993). Roman Catholic communion preparation course for children. Also Parents/Catechist's book.

Harding, Nick, *Share: A Communion Preparation Course for 7–11s* (Stowmarket, Kevin Mayhew, 2002). Short preparation course for use with children, and sessions for parents/carers too. Out of print, but copies may be available from your diocesan office.

Leichner, Jeannine Timko, *Our Sunday Visitor* (Huntington, IN: Our Sunday Visitor, 2007). Catechist's Roman Catholic communion preparation course from the United States. Children's book also available.

Murrie, Diana, *Children and Holy Communion: A Creative Preparation Programme* (Stowmarket: Kevin Mayhew, 2008). Very good basic introduction with a simple, six-part preparation session.

Urquart, Aileen, *I Belong: Leader's Guide* (Chawton: Redemptorist Publications, 1999). Leader's Guide for a Roman Catholic communion preparation course. Children's and parents' books are also available.

Withers, Margaret, *Welcome to the Lord's Table: A Practical Course for Preparing Children to Receive Holy Communion* (Abingdon: Bible Reading Fellowship, 2006). Communion preparation course for six- to eleven-year-olds. A children's activity book is also available.

Withers, Margaret and Tim Sledge, *Creative Communion: Engaging the Whole Church in a Journey of Faith* (Abingdon: Bible Reading Fellowship, 2008). Workshops and preparation to help the whole church think through aspects of communion.

Liturgical resources

Harding, Nick, *All-age Everything: All You Ever Wanted to Know about All-age Worship* (Stowmarket: Kevin Mayhew, 2001). A book full of liturgical worship resources – greetings, confessions, creeds, intercessions, blessings, visuals and so on – that are interactive and designed for all-age worship.

McCann, Julie, *Spiritual Garments* (Brandon: Decani Books, 2006). Written to help Roman Catholic primary teachers know and understand liturgy. Very good, practical book on leading worship with children and helping children become leaders of worship.

Millar, Sandra, *Worship Together: Creating All-age Services that Work* (London: SPCK, 2012). A guide to the theory and practice of creating worship that really works for everyone. Includes 12 tried-and-tested all-age service outlines, one for each month of the year.

Millar, Sandra, *Festivals Together: Creating All-age Worship Through the Year* (London: SPCK, 2012). A companion volume to *Worship Together*. Contains 15 services for occasions throughout the church year, including Christmas Day, Mothering Sunday, Easter Sunday, Pentecost, Father's Day, Harvest and Remembrance.

Nicholls, Rachel, *The Feast is Ready to Begin* (Stowmarket, Kevin Mayhew, 2009). A book on all-age Eucharist based on *Common Worship*. Fourteen outlines following the church year, with very good 'how to' material in the Introduction.

School Eucharists

Jumping Fish school Eucharist resources: see <gloucester.anglican.org/schools/jumping-fish-publications/>.

Prayer Spaces in Schools: see <www.prayerspacesinschools.com>.